CELEBRATING OUR MOTHERS' KITCHENS

**TREASURED
MEMORIES**
AND
**TESTED
RECIPES**

The National Council of Negro Women, Inc.

Copyright ©1994 by The National Council of Negro Women, Inc.

Published by The Wimmer Companies, Inc., Memphis, Tennessee,
in corporate partnership with

KRAFT GENERAL FOODS

with special appreciation to Cheryl Whiteman-Brooks, Manager KGF Ethnic
Marketing and the GFUSA Test Kitchen for their efforts in recipe
development and testing. ANGEL FLAKE, BAKER'S, BRAN'NOLA, CERTO,
COOL WHIP, GOLDEN CRISP, GOOD SEASONS, GRAPE-NUTS, JELL-O,
KRAFT, KOOL-AID, LOG CABIN, MAXWELL HOUSE, MINUTE,
OSCAR MAYER, PARKAY, PHILADELPHIA BRAND, POST, SANKA,
SHAKE 'N BAKE, STOVE TOP and VELVEETA are trademarks of
Kraft General Foods, Inc.

All Rights Reserved

This book, or any portions thereof, may not be reproduced in any form
without written permission of the publisher, The Wimmer Companies, Inc.

TRADERY
H·O·U·S·E

First Printing   June, 1994
Second Printing   September, 1994
Third Printing   November, 1994
Fourth Printing   February, 1995
Fifth Printing   May, 1995
Sixth Printing   January, 1996
Seventh Printing   June, 1996
Eighth Printing   April, 1997

Printed in the United States of America by The Wimmer Companies, Inc.
Memphis, Tennessee

Library of Congress Cataloging-in-Publication Data
Celebrating our mothers' kitchens: treasured memories and tested recipes
p. cm.
Includes index.
ISBN 1-879958-23-6: $15.95
1. Afro-American cookery. I. National Council of Negro Women.
TX715.C3514 1994
641.59'296073--dc20   04-18488
                                                                      CIP

Any inquiries should be directed to
The National Council of Negro Women, Inc.
1001 G Street, NW, Suite 800, Washington, DC 20001

For additional copies, use the order forms at the back of the book or call:

The Wimmer Companies, Inc.
1-800-727-1034

TABLE OF CONTENTS

DEDICATION

This very special cookbook pays tribute to the creative relationships, the warmth of connections made with each other and the truths shared around the kitchen table even as African American mothers prepared the family meal. I dedicate this book

To my own mother,
whose gentle but firm example and words of wisdom instilled values that have sustained me through the years.

To Mary McLeod Bethune,
affectionately called "Ma Bethune" by the many inspired by her example to work for others and not themselves alone.

To the Mothers of the Women of Distinction,
Their daughters are representatives of those who exemplify the highest ideals and enduring strengths that have made them who they are.

To the Unity in Our Diversity
that intrigues us to create recipes, kitchen secrets and memories and come in touch with the value traditions and experiences that have nourished the bodies and spirits of the African American family for generations presented in *Celebrating Our Mothers' Kitchens.*

Dorothy I. Height
President & CEO,
The National Council of Negro Women, Inc.

ACKNOWLEDGEMENTS

The original pastel created for the cover, *Kitchen Conference*, is the work of **BRENDA JOYSMITH**, "one of the nation's most acclaimed young artists" according to the late Alex Haley. Ms. Joysmith is a native of Memphis, Tennessee and a current resident of San Francisco. Her work has received national exposure on the sets of such popular television shows as *The Cosby Show, A Different World, Amen, Family Matters* and *Sinbad*. Her Joysmith Studio, specializing in publishing, marketing and distribution of African-American art, services over 700 retailers and galleries nationally.

JESSICA B. HARRIS, a recognized authority on African-American cooking, was editorial consultant for the project. She wrote the introduction and annotations for the heritage recipes. She lives in New York City and is a professor of French and English at Queens College. She is the author of five cookbooks including *Hot Stuff: In Praise of the Piquant, Iron Pots & Wooden Spoons: Africa's Gift to New World Cooking* and *Sky Juice & Flying Fish: Traditional Caribbean Cooking, Tasting Brazil: Regional Recipes & Reminiscences* and forthcoming titles, *From Quingombo to Gumbo: African American Heritage Cooking* and *Nyam: A History of African American Foodways*.

GFUSA TEST KITCHENS, which tested all recipes from NCNW members to ensure successful preparation for readers and to help document and preserve authentic African American cooking techniques and customs.

CELEBRATING OUR MOTHERS' KITCHENS

The rich molassesy smells of pralines cooking in a saucepan waft their way through the house. The pungent aroma of a slow-cooked pot of smoked pork and greens vies with the fragrance of a clove-studded baked ham and the steam from a pot of Hoppin' John to perfume the air on a New Year's morning. The quiet persistent bubbling of a homemade soup as it simmers on the back of the stove on a cold winter afternoon provides a counterpoint to family conversations, while the insistent snapping and popping of chicken frying in a cast-iron skillet marks time. Mama's in the kitchen and it's home. These smells and sounds are imbedded in our fiber as much as our other family traits. These sensory memories are a part of our communal heritage and our personal past.

Throughout the country, whether in New York or New Orleans, Raleigh or Rochester, Detroit or Dallas, San Francisco or Savannah, hands the color of nutmegs, saffron, ginger, vanilla and coffee have stirred pots, heated skillets, fed families on food and food for thought for generations.

Mama in the kitchen is emblematic of all the nurturing and the warmth of mothering. The mere thought of Mama standing over the stove or waiting at the doorway calling, "Supper's ready!" brings with it a host of other images: helping hands still floured with biscuit dough, tousled hair disarranged by steam, and slightly damp faces that radiate the heat of the stove back with the additional warmth from that invisible ingredient known as love. These are the mothers who carried us over and got us through — the women whose love and advice made us who and what we are today. These are the generations of mothers stretching back over time who, from their kitchen kingdoms, dispensed their knowledge of the world, their strategies for survival, and their hopes for the future, along with airy angel biscuits, succulent smothered pork chops, and bubbling pots of homemade soup. Their warmth is the warmth of our Mother's kitchen.

More than any other room of the house, the kitchen is the heart of the home, the heartbeat of the house. It's the soul and life force of the family. The warmth of the kitchen is the warmth of our mothers and grandmothers. The center of family life, the kitchen was traditionally where hair was done and homework corrected. It's where family came together. Whatever its size and decor, more than any other room in the house, the kitchen is invested with the weight of tradition and the life lessons learned from mothers past — lessons which are to be transmitted to mothers future.

Author Paule Marshall, in an essay entitled "Poets in the Kitchen," reveals that she first learned the power of language sitting around the kitchen table, listening to her Mother and her friends discussing their lives as domestic workers in Brooklyn. Others of us learned everything from our mothers from negotiating skills to recipes while resting on unmatched chairs and sipping a cool drink out of jelly jar glasses.

The power of the kitchen is in its informality. It's where tall tales can be told with ease, where family gossip is taken out and gnawed on, along with the bones of the chicken carcass. It's where meals and feelings are re-heated and served up anew. In short, it's where life is savored as languorously and lovingly as that last hot cup of coffee, the final bit of bacon, and the ultimate biscuit at Sunday breakfast.

Even today, when the kitchen may be no more than a closet-sized room with a hot plate and microwave, the kitchen is more than simply a room of memories. It's where life lessons are learned, where tears may be shed and dried, and where family comes together. The locus of the most intimate of family moments, the kitchen is a bridge between the past and the future, the place where we bring the lessons learned from our grandmothers and our mothers to the next generation.

As we look toward the 21st century, far too many of us are losing this warmth and this communion. The family experience of mealtime is disappearing under the weight of multiple mealtimes. Today's family rarely sits down together. Cramped spaces of yesterday's kitchen table are being replaced by trays in another room in front of blaring television sets that halt all mealtime exchanges; family members eat at different times due to work schedules; and confrontations replace conversations. However, these trappings of modern life should not allow us to lose the amazing nurturing power of mealtime communion.

Now, when all will agree that many of society's ills stem from the breaking up of the family unit, we should look to the past as a help for the future. Whether the family is a single parent household or a gaggle of gossiping relatives clustered around a table, turn back the hands of time at least one day a week. Silence the television set; sit down together; take time to discuss, listen, exchange, advise, and share. It's sure to help. It would be naive to assume that the ills of the present can be healed by a return to the past. However, they can surely be salved and perhaps eased with the gentle application of the balm of a Mother's love and advice, the healing communion of family, and the timeless, sustaining warmth of our Mother's kitchen.

Jessica B. Harris

WOMEN OF DISTINCTION

MY MOTHER, THELMA WATTS, SAID...

*M*any of the most important talks of my life took place in Mama's kitchen. That's where her strong hands would chop and snap and rinse and stir — and where her strong voice was heard over the simmer of the family stew. A voice of wisdom in total command. Even on those days when she would explain why she could not allow me to try out for "beauty queen this" or "cheerleader that."

"I want you to be known for your brains," she would say with a stern stare straight into my eyes,"…and if you want to bounce on the field, then get in the game."

"Git in the game?" my only reply.

"No, get there," she'd correct, "not 'git,' get! G-E-T, get! Remember, you must also speak well and pronounce your words correctly, like 'get'…because one day you might want to 'get' a job!"

Because of Mama's stews, she nourished my body. Because of Mama's words, she nourished my soul. And because of Mama's lessons, in Mama's kitchen, Mama prepared more than a dinner. She also prepared a daughter to be a woman in the game of "getting" jobs for speaking well.

Rolonda Watts
Television and Talk Show Personality

CELEBRATING
OUR
MOTHERS'
SOUPS &
SALADS

ROSIE'S BEST CREOLE GUMBO

8 **cups water**
3½ **pounds chicken pieces**
2 **stalks celery, chopped**
1 **large onion, chopped**
1 **green pepper, chopped**
1 **cup chopped green onions**
1 **jalapeño pepper, minced**
2 **teaspoons pepper**
2 **teaspoons salt**
1 **teaspoon ground red pepper**
⅓ **cup oil**
¾ **cup flour**
1 **can (28 ounces) whole peeled tomatoes, cut up**
1 **pound kielbasa, sliced**
1 **package (10 ounces) frozen cut okra**
1 **pound large shrimp, cleaned**
½ **pound fresh crabmeat**
2 **tablespoons filé powder**
 Hot cooked rice

Bring water, chicken, vegetables and spices to boil in large saucepot. Reduce heat to low; cover and simmer 40 minutes or until chicken is tender. Remove chicken; cool slightly. Remove skin and bones. Return chicken to pot; discard skin and bones.

Meanwhile, heat oil in large skillet on low heat. Stir in flour. Stirring constantly, cook 25 minutes or until dark brown but not burned. Gradually stir flour mixture into saucepot. Add tomatoes, kielbasa and okra; return to boil. Reduce heat to low; cover and simmer 15 minutes.

Add shrimp and crabmeat; cook 5 minutes or until shrimp are pink. Stir in filé; cook 2 minutes. Serve over rice.

Makes 18 servings.

HERITAGE RECIPE

MY MOTHER LEONA EDWARDS MCCAULEY SAID...

"When I had a difficult task, my mother would gently say, 'Keep inching along like a poor inch worm. You will get there by and by.'"

Rosa L. Parks
Civil Rights Activist

OXTAIL SOUP

2	tablespoons oil
2	pounds oxtails, cut into 1½-inch pieces
1	medium onion, chopped
1	clove garlic, minced
4	cups water
1	can (28 ounces) whole tomatoes, cut up
1	can (8 ounces) tomato sauce
2	teaspoons salt
¼	teaspoon pepper
1	package (10 ounces) frozen mixed vegetables
½	cup small shell pasta, cooked, drained

Heat oil in large saucepot on medium high heat. Brown oxtails on all sides, removing from pan as they brown. Add onion and garlic to saucepot; cook and stir until tender.

Return oxtails to pot. Add water, tomatoes, tomato sauce, salt and pepper; bring to boil. Reduce heat to low; cover and simmer 3 hours or until meat is very tender. Remove oxtails from pot; cool slightly. Remove meat from bones. Shred meat. Return to pot; discard bones.

Add mixed vegetables; cook 5 minutes or until vegetables are tender. Stir in pasta.

Makes 6 servings.

♥ NEVER TASTE FOOD WITH YOUR "COOKING SPOON" BECAUSE BACTERIA WILL GET IN AND SPOIL THE WHOLE POT.

MY MOTHER ALTHEA HUNTER SAID...

My Mother told me not to worry about my classmates and friends teasing me about having the largest feet in my group. "Just tell them," she said, "the bigger the foot, the firmer the foundation."

Charlayne Hunter-Gault
National Correspondent, The MacNeil/Lehrer Newshour

MOMMIE'S SPLIT PEA SOUP

1 **package (16 ounces) dry green split peas**
8 **cups water**
1 **pound chicken backs***
2 **carrots, chopped**
1 **medium onion, chopped**
2 **celery stalks, chopped**
2½ **teaspoons salt**
2 **tablespoons quick-cooking oats**
Hot cooked rice and cornbread

Or use smoked ham hocks and reduce salt to 1½ teaspoons.

Rinse and soak peas as directed on package.

Bring peas, water, chicken, carrots, celery, onion and salt to boil in large saucepot. Reduce heat to low; cover and simmer 2 hours.

Stir in oats; cook 5 minutes. Remove chicken; cool slightly. Remove chicken from bones. Return to pot; discard bones. Serve with rice and cornbread.

Makes 6 servings.

MY MOTHER MATTIE "SUGAR" DAVIS SAID...
"The Lord gave you Ten Commandments, not ten suggestions."
Jessie Davis Walls
Bronx, NY

PEANUT BUTTER SOUP
WITH CHICKEN

2 tablespoons oil
4 boneless skinless chicken breast halves, cut into ½-inch chunks
1 large onion, finely chopped
1 jalapeño pepper, minced
2 cups water, divided
2 tablespoons creamy peanut butter
1 large tomato, finely chopped
1 teaspoon salt
Hot cooked rice

Heat oil in large saucepot on medium-high heat. Add chicken; brown on all sides, removing pieces as they brown. Add onion and pepper; cook and stir until tender.

Gradually stir ⅓ cup of the water into the peanut butter in small bowl until smooth. Return chicken to pot. Add remaining 1⅔ cups water, peanut butter mixture, tomato and salt; bring to boil. Reduce heat to low; cover and simmer 20 minutes. Serve over rice or as a soup.

Makes 4 servings.

MAMA DEAN'S SUPER SOUP

8 cups water
4 boneless skinless chicken breast halves
3 carrots, diced
2 stalks celery, diced
¼ cup chopped onion
2 chicken bouillon cubes
1½ teaspoons salt
1 cup frozen peas
½ cup frozen corn
2 cups noodles, uncooked

Bring water, chicken, carrots, celery, onion, bouillon cubes and salt to boil in large saucepot. Reduce heat to low; cover and simmer 15 minutes or until chicken is tender. Remove chicken; cool slightly. Shred chicken. Return to pot. Add peas and corn; bring to boil. Add noodles; reduce heat to low. Simmer, uncovered, 8 minutes or until noodles are tender.

Makes 4 servings.

GUMBO

Dip a spoon into a steaming, hot bowl of gumbo and you can almost hear the sounds of a Dixie land jazz band warming up. Taste it and your feet begin to tap, itching to "second line" down a New Orleans street. Finish it and you know that you've just savored one of the classic dishes of African-American cooking.

Gumbo, southern Louisiana's gift to the world, has close relatives in the foods of Africa and the New World. The soupy stew is prepared using a variety of ingredients ranging from duck or chicken, which is frequently paired with the spicy sausage known as andouille, to the bounty of the Gulf of Mexico: crayfish, shrimp, oysters, and more. The whole is thickened with a generous measure of okra or with the powdered leaves of the sassafras plant known as filé. The result is ambrosial.

The varieties of gumbo are infinite, and ingredients are defined by the region and the inventiveness of the cook. New Orleans and southern Louisiana natives will spend hours arguing over the relative merits of uptown versus downtown, Cajun versus Creole, okra versus filé gumbo. Other folks just sit back and taste and savor, knowing that whatever the gumbo...ooh, it's just so go-o-o-o-d!

—Jessica B. Harris

MY MOTHER ANNETTE LEWIS HOAGE PHINAZEE, PH.D., SAID...

"Be efficient. Take time to plan a 'system' before you begin a project. Put your clothes up as soon as you take them off. Try to get to the point where you handle a piece of correspondence only once. Think efficiency!"

Ramona H. Edelin
President/CEO
National Urban Coalition

CHICKEN GUMBO WITH RICE

2 tablespoons margarine or butter
1 medium onion, chopped
1 stalk celery, chopped
1 small green pepper, chopped
1 package (16 ounces) frozen blackeye peas
4 cups chicken broth
1 tablespoon lemon juice
1½ teaspoons salt
1 teaspoon Worcestershire sauce
¼ teaspoon pepper
1 bay leaf
2 cups diced cooked chicken
1 package (10 ounces) frozen corn
½ pound okra, sliced
Hot cooked rice

Melt margarine in large saucepan on medium-high heat. Add onion, celery and green pepper; cook and stir until onion is tender. Add peas, broth, lemon juice and seasonings; bring to boil. Reduce heat to low; cover and simmer 45 minutes.

Add chicken, corn and okra; return to boil, stirring occasionally. Reduce heat to low; cover and simmer 6 minutes or until okra and corn are tender. Remove bay leaf. Serve with rice.

Makes 12 servings.

HERITAGE RECIPE

MY MOTHER GUSSIE G. WALKER SAID...

"Never let your emotions run away with your better judgment."

Grace Walker Phillips
Silver Spring, MD

VEGETABLE STEW

Wash day was usually Friday at our house, and that was the day we had vegetable stew for dinner. We also had it during the fall and winter when we came in from school. The pot was there on the stove, and we knew that there was going to be vegetable stew for dinner. We knew that this was a dish that would be served whenever my Mother was going to be busy. My Mother was very popular for her one dish meals. As time went on and we got refrigeration, she'd save a jar full of all of our leftover vegetables, and, when there were enough, we'd have Vegetable Stew. The stew was a way of stretching things and not wasting. My Mother was very simple and very practical, and I think she instilled those qualities in me.

—**Stella Fleming Hughes**
St. Louis, Missouri

MOTHER'S VEGETABLE STEW

4 cups water
1 pound smoked ham bones or smoked ham hocks
1 medium onion, chopped
1 clove garlic, minced
1 can (17 ounces) whole kernel corn, drained
1 can (16 ounces) whole peeled tomatoes, cut up
1 package (10 ounces) frozen cut okra
1 teaspoon dried basil leaves
1 teaspoon sugar
½ teaspoon salt
¼ teaspoon pepper
Corn bread or crusty French bread

Bring water, ham, onion and garlic to boil in large saucepot. Reduce heat to low; cover and simmer 2 hours or until ham is tender. Remove ham; cool slightly. Cut ham from bones. Return to pot; discard bones.

Add corn, tomatoes, okra, basil, sugar, salt and pepper; return to boil. Reduce heat to low; simmer, uncovered, 10 minutes or until okra is tender, stirring occasionally. Serve with corn bread or French bread.

Makes 4 servings.

MAFFE

½ cup oil
3 pounds chicken pieces
3 medium onions, diced
2½ cups boiling water
⅔ cup creamy peanut butter
2 tablespoons tomato paste
4 medium tomatoes, peeled, diced
3 carrots, chopped
2 sweet potatoes, peeled, cut into 2-inch cubes
2 jalapeño peppers, finely chopped
1 teaspoon salt
Dash ground cinnamon
Dash paprika
1½ cups frozen whole kernel corn
1 cup fresh or frozen cut okra
Hot cooked rice

Heat oil in large saucepot on medium-high heat. Add chicken; brown on both sides. Remove chicken. Add onions; cook and stir until tender.

Stir water, peanut butter and tomato paste in medium bowl until well blended; add to saucepot.

Stir in chicken, tomatoes, carrots, sweet potatoes, peppers, salt, cinnamon and paprika to saucepot; bring to boil. Reduce heat to low; cover and simmer 40 minutes or until chicken is tender.

Add corn and okra; cook, covered, 8 minutes or until vegetables are tender. Serve over rice.

Makes 6 servings.

MY MOTHER LEONA LOWE-COLEMAN SAID...

"Love everyone...Some because of and some in spite of."

Dorothy Durden-Thompson
Cleveland Heights, OH

VEGETARIAN CHILI

1	tablespoon oil
1½	cups finely chopped onions
2	green peppers, sliced
3	carrots, thinly sliced
1	teaspoon minced garlic
2	cans (15½ ounces each) red kidney beans, drained and rinsed (3 cups)
1	can (8 ounces) peeled tomatoes, undrained
1	can (4 ounces) chopped green chilies, undrained
5	cups 100% vegetable juice
1¼	teaspoons chili powder
1	teaspoon dried oregano leaves
1	teaspoon ground cumin
½	teaspoon salt
¼	teaspoon pepper

Heat oil in large skillet on medium heat. Add onions, green peppers, carrots and garlic; cook and stir until tender. Stir in beans, tomatoes, chilies, juice and seasonings until well blended; cover. Cook 25 to 30 minutes.

Makes 8½ cups.
Dr. Jeanne L. Noble
Professor,
The City University of New York

MY MOTHER MYRTLE DAVIS SAID...

"Pay as you go and you will never owe."

Shirley Ann Davis Morris
Cleveland, MS

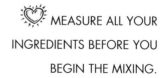 MEASURE ALL YOUR INGREDIENTS BEFORE YOU BEGIN THE MIXING.

CHILI À LA ALMETTA

1	**pound ground beef**
1	**small onion, chopped**
1	**clove garlic, minced**
3	**tablespoons chili powder**
1	**can (28 ounces) whole tomatoes with puree**
1	**teaspoon salt**
1	**teaspoon sugar**
¼	**teaspoon ground cumin**
¼	**teaspoon ground red pepper**
⅛	**teaspoon pepper**
	Dash hot pepper sauce
2	**tablespoons yellow cornmeal**
	Hot cooked rice

Brown beef, onion and garlic in large skillet; drain. Add chili powder; cook 1 minute.

Stir in tomatoes, salt, sugar, cumin, ground pepper and pepper sauce; bring to boil. Reduce heat to low; cover and simmer 10 minutes. Stir in cornmeal. Serve over rice.

Makes 4 servings.

MY MOTHER HENIETTA "MOMA" RETTA YATES SAID...

"If you make your bed hard, you have to lay in it! What you choose to do in life, you have to live with your choices."

Carol Yates-Bennett
Maysville, KY

CORN CHOWDER

10 ears fresh corn
1 tablespoon oil
1 smoked turkey wing
8 cups chicken broth
1 cup diced celery
1 cup diced carrots
1 cup diced potato
1 cup finely chopped onion
  Salt and pepper
2 cups cream
  Chopped fresh parsley

Slice corn kernels from cob into bowl. Scrape remaining part of kernels and milk from cob, using back of knife, scraping downward into bowl; reserve.

Heat oil in large saucepot over medium heat. Add turkey; cook turning frequently until cooked through. Remove turkey; cool slightly. Remove turkey from bones. Cut into small pieces; reserve. Discard bones.

Add broth, reserved corn mixture, celery, carrots, potatoes and onions to pot; cover. Bring to boil. Reduce heat to low; simmer 25 minutes or until vegetables are tender. Season with salt and pepper. Stir in cream. Cook until hot. DO NOT BOIL. Ladle into bowls. Garnish with reserved turkey and parsley.

Makes 6 servings.
Patti LaBelle
Queen of Rock 'n Soul

MY MOTHER BERTHA HOLTE SAID...

Though a lot of people find it hard to believe, there's a part of me that will always be that shy little girl — afraid to take her steps into the big world — just like there's a part of me that will always see my kitchen as a safe haven. But thanks to my Mother I learned how to reach out to others. I learned the real joy of making my place in the world. And when I'm in my kitchen cooking dinner for my sons and husband, or even scrubbing that oven, I do it wrapped in the love of my Mother.

Patti LaBelle
Queen of Rock 'n Soul

CABBAGE & BEAN SOUP

1 package (16 ounces) dry navy beans
5 quarts water
1 smoked ham hock
2 tablespoons olive oil
3 ounces thick-sliced bacon, cut into small pieces
2 large bulbs fennel, chopped*
2 large onions, chopped
2 large carrots, chopped
3 cloves garlic, chopped
1 teaspoon salt
1 bay leaf
1 teaspoon ground cumin
1 teaspoon dried oregano leaves
½ teaspoon crushed red pepper
2 small potatoes, diced
1 head cabbage, shredded
½ cup grated Parmesan cheese

*Use only the white part of the fennel.

Rinse and soak beans as directed on package.

Bring beans, water and ham to boil in large saucepot. Reduce heat to low; cover and simmer 1½ hours or until ham and beans are tender.

Meanwhile, heat oil in large skillet on medium heat. Add bacon, fennel, onions, carrots, garlic and seasonings; cook and stir until vegetables are tender. Add cooked vegetable mixture, potatoes and cabbage to saucepot; simmer 30 minutes, adding additional water if necessary. Sprinkle with cheese.

Makes 15 servings.
Barbara Bond
Barbara's Bounty,
Cincinnati, Ohio

MY MOTHER IRENE VIRGINIA TOWE SELLS SAID...

"Never stop studying. There is so much to learn. Prepare yourself to do many things so that you will be able to walk in when the door of opportunity knocks."

Rose Elizabeth Sells Rhetta
Alton, IL

COLE SLAW

My Mother made this later on as we were older. I was a diabetic, but I didn't know that then. None of us knew about her "trick." She only told us in later years, just before she passed on, that she used Sweet and Low in place of sugar in her cole slaw. The cole slaw is delicious. Once I learned about it from my Mom, I started making it. Now I bring it to all of the family gatherings. Each of us is supposed to bring what we make best, and I make the best cole slaw. Even though it can be great for some people with diabetes, the whole family loves it.

Joan Odom
New York, New York

SWEET & SASSY COLE SLAW

- **1 cup Kraft real mayonnaise**
- **2 tablespoons cider vinegar**
- **1 tablespoon sugar***
- **1½ teaspoons salt**
- **½ teaspoon pepper**
- **4 cups shredded cabbage**
- **4 cups shredded red cabbage**
- **1 large cucumber, shredded**
- **1 red or green pepper, cut into strips**
- **2 large carrots, shredded**
- **1 small onion, finely chopped**

Or substitute non-nutritive sweetener to taste.

Stir mayonnaise, vinegar, sugar, salt and pepper in small bowl. Toss cabbages, cucumber, red pepper, carrots and onion in large bowl. Add salad dressing mixture; toss to coat. Cover.

Refrigerate at least 1 hour, stirring occasionally. Stir in additional mayonnaise, if desired.

Makes 10 servings.

APPLE-PINEAPPLE COLESLAW

¾ cup **Kraft real mayonnaise**
1 teaspoon **salt**
¼ teaspoon **pepper**
3 cups **shredded cabbage**
1 large **apple, diced**
1 can (8 ounces) **crushed pineapple in juice, undrained**
1 cup **Kraft miniature marshmallows (optional)**
1 stalk **celery, diced**
Apple wedges

Stir mayonnaise, salt and pepper in small bowl. Mix cabbage, apple, pineapple, marshmallows and celery in large bowl. Add mayonnaise mixture; toss to coat. Cover.

Refrigerate at least 1 hour, stirring occasionally. Stir in additional mayonnaise, if desired. Garnish with apple wedges.

Makes 10 servings.

SOUTHERN-STYLE AMBROSIA

3 large **oranges**
2 **bananas, sliced**
½ **pineapple, peeled, cored and diced**
1 package (7 ounces) **Baker's Angel Flake coconut**
Maraschino cherries

Peel oranges over large bowl reserving juice. Dice oranges. Add oranges, bananas and pineapple to bowl. Gently stir in coconut; cover.

Refrigerate several hours or until serving. Garnish with cherries.

Makes 12 servings.

Tanzanian Ambrosia: Prepare as directed, stirring in ½ cup light cream, ¼ cup coarsely chopped salted cashews, 2 tablespoons honey and 1 to 2 tablespoons rum with the coconut.

MY MOTHER SARAH A. CHAMPION SAID...

"Stay out of people's way that have a problem and you will not have one."

Richard John Champion
East Point, GA

BETHUNE FRUIT SALAD

Sauce:
- 1 container (16 ounces) sour cream
- 1 cup firmly packed brown sugar
- Juice of 1 orange
- Juice of ½ lemon
- 3 tablespoons pineapple juice
- 1 teaspoon cinnamon

Fruit Salad:
- 1 cup cubed cantaloupe
- 1 cup cubed honeydew melon
- 1 cup cubed fresh pineapple
- 2 peaches, sliced
- ½ pound seedless grapes, whole or halved lengthwise
- 2 oranges, peeled, sliced
- 1 can (11 ounces) mandarin orange segments, drained
- 2 bananas, sliced
- Maraschino cherries (optional)

For sauce, stir sour cream, sugar, juices and cinnamon in medium bowl; cover and refrigerate until ready to serve.

For fruit salad, mix melons, pineapple, peaches, grapes and oranges in large bowl; cover.

Refrigerate until ready to serve. Stir bananas into fruit mixture. Spoon into individual serving dishes. Top with sauce. Garnish with cherries.

Makes 14 servings.
Delia Johnson, Caterer
Johnson's Catering

MY MOTHER RUBY DAVIS LANDCASTER SAID...

"Always have carfare and change to make a phone call in case of trouble." This was how she contemporized the old adage "God Bless the child that has 'her' own."

Nola Lancaster Whiteman
Brooklyn, NY

WEST INDIES CRAB SALAD

1 **small onion, finely chopped**
2 **tablespoons oil**
2 **tablespoons cold water**
1½ **tablespoons cider vinegar**
1 **bay leaf**
¼ **teaspoon salt**
⅛ **teaspoon pepper**
2 **cans (6 ounces each) crabmeat, drained, flaked* Red leaf lettuce, lemon wedges and parsley**

*Or use ½ pound fresh crabmeat, flaked.

Mix onion, oil, water, vinegar, bay leaf, salt and pepper in large bowl. Gently stir in crab; cover.

Refrigerate at least 1 hour. Remove bay leaf. Using slotted spoon, spoon onto 4 lettuce-lined plates. Garnish with lemon wedges and parsley.

Makes 4 servings.

PICNIC MACARONI SALAD

1 **package (14 ounces) Kraft deluxe macaroni & cheese dinner**
¾ **cup Kraft sandwich spread**
½ **cup chopped celery**
½ **cup chopped cucumber**
½ **cup chopped red or green pepper**
⅓ **cup sliced green onions**

Prepare dinner as directed on package. Add remaining ingredients; mix well.

Refrigerate until ready to serve. Stir in additional sandwich spread before serving, if desired.

Makes 8 servings.

TABOULI

1 cup bulgur*
2 cups water*
2 large tomatoes, diced
1 can (19 ounces) garbanzo beans, drained
1 cup finely chopped parsley
1 bunch green onions, thinly sliced
½ cup chopped fresh mint
1 envelope Good Seasons garlic and herb salad dressing mix
¼ cup lemon juice
2 tablespoons water
½ cup oil

*Or use 2 cups Minute brown rice prepared as directed on package.

Prepare bulgur with water as directed on package; drain, if necessary.

Mix bulgur, tomatoes, beans, parsley, onions and mint in large bowl. Prepare salad dressing mix with lemon juice, water and oil as directed on envelope. Add dressing to bulgur mixture; toss to coat. Cover.

Refrigerate until ready to serve, stirring occasionally.

Makes 6 servings.

MY MOTHER LOUISE B. MILLER SAID...

"Faith in God will enable you to face any challenge."

Christine Toney
Washington, DC

POTATO SALAD

One of the favorite treats of summer is the creamy taste of potatoes with a hint of celery and a taste of onion. It may show up on the dining table elaborately molded or served simply in a refrigerator container, but it will be there. No summer picnic, barbecue, fish fry, or family reunion held between May 30th and Labor Day would be complete without a dish of potato salad occupying the place of honor on the groaning board.

Like catching fireflies and going to the beach, potato salad is basically just a part of our summer life. (We eat it in the winter, too, but it just seems to go with summer like picnics and barbecues.)

There are undoubtedly many schools of thought on making potato salad ranging from the minimal to the put-it-all-in school, which adds everything from hard-cooked eggs to red and green bell peppers. The only criterion is that the flavors must blend perfectly in an explosion of tastes. Great potato salad does all of this and more. It takes us all back to the simpler summers of long ago, to the times of cool drinks in frosty pitchers, of hot grills, and warm gatherings of family and friends.

—Jessica B. Harris

MAMA'S POTATO SALAD

1½ **cups Kraft real mayonnaise**
1 **cup sweet pickle relish**
2 **tablespoons Dijon mustard**
1 **teaspoon salt**
½ **teaspoon pepper Dash hot pepper sauce**
4 **large cubed peeled cooked potatoes, cooled**
3 **hard-cooked eggs, chopped**
1 **medium green pepper, chopped**
2 **medium carrots, shredded**
2 **stalks celery, chopped**
1 **small onion, grated**

Mix mayonnaise, relish, mustard, salt, pepper and hot pepper sauce in large bowl. Gently stir in potatoes, eggs, green pepper, carrots, celery and onion; cover.

Refrigerate at least 2 hours, stirring occasionally. Stir in additional mayonnaise, if desired. Garnish with paprika and parsley sprigs.

Makes 12 servings.

HERITAGE RECIPE

ROASTED POTATO SALAD

4 cups quartered unpeeled small red potatoes
1 cup Miracle Whip salad dressing
4 slices Oscar Mayer bacon, chopped, crisply cooked, drained
2 hard-cooked eggs, chopped
¼ cup sliced green onions
¼ teaspoon salt
¼ teaspoon pepper

Heat oven to 425°F.

Place potatoes on 15x10x1-inch baking pan sprayed with no stick cooking spray.

Bake 30 to 35 minutes or until potatoes are tender and golden brown, stirring once. Cool slightly.

Mix dressing, bacon, eggs, onions, salt and pepper in large bowl. Add potatoes; mix lightly. Serve warm or chilled. Stir in additional salad dressing, if desired.

Makes 6 servings.

PASTA SALAD

1 package (12 ounces) tricolored rotini, uncooked
1 large tomato, diced
1 large red onion, diced
1 stalk celery, diced
1 envelope Good Seasons zesty Italian salad dressing mix
¼ cup vinegar
2 tablespoons water
½ cup oil

Prepare pasta as directed on package; drain. Rinse under cold water to cool; drain well. Toss pasta with tomato, onion and celery in large bowl.

Prepare salad dressing mix with vinegar, water and oil as directed on envelope. Add dressing to pasta mixture; toss to coat. Cover.

Refrigerate at least 2 hours or until ready to serve, stirring occasionally.

Makes 10 servings.

MY MOTHER OLIVE EAVES YOUNG SAID...
"There is a light inside you greater than any problem."
Patricia Gibson
Washington, DC

SPICED CRANBERRY-ORANGE MOLD

1 **bag (12 ounces) fresh cranberries***

½ **cup sugar***

1½ **cups boiling water**

1 **package (8-serving size) or 2 packages (4-serving size) Jell-O brand orange or lemon flavor gelatin**

¼ **teaspoon salt (optional)**

1 **cup cold water***

1 **tablespoon lemon juice**

¼ **teaspoon ground cinnamon**

⅛ **teaspoon ground cloves**

1 **orange, sectioned, diced**

½ **chopped nuts**

Or use 1 can (16 ounces) whole berry cranberry sauce, omit sugar and reduce water to ½ cup.

Spray 5-cup mold with no stick cooking spray. Place on large tray for easy transfer to refrigerator.

Finely chop cranberries in food processor; mix with sugar. Set aside.

Stir boiling water into gelatin and salt in large bowl 2 minutes or until completely dissolved. Stir in cold water, lemon juice, cinnamon and cloves. Refrigerate 1½ hours or until thickened (spoon drawn through leaves a definite impression).

Stir in cranberries, orange and nuts. Spoon into prepared mold.

Refrigerate about 4 hours or until firm. Unmold. Garnish as desired.

Makes 10 servings.

MY MOTHER MARGARET GIRTON O'NEAL SAID...

"Prepare every dish with care and love — no recipe can go wrong with those ingredients."

Brenda Girton
Washington, DC

CARROT & OLIVE SALAD

1 cup boiling water
1 package
(4-serving size)
Jell-O brand
lemon flavor
gelatin*
½ teaspoon salt
¾ cup cold water
1 tablespoon
vinegar
1 cup shredded
carrots
¼ cup diced celery
¼ cup sliced green
olives

*Or use Jell-O brand
lemon flavor sugar
free low calorie
gelatin.*

Stir boiling water into gelatin and salt in large bowl 2 minutes or until completely dissolved. Stir in cold water and vinegar. Refrigerate 1½ hours or until thickened (spoon drawn through leaves a definite impression).

Stir in carrots, celery and olives. Spoon into 3-cup mold or bowl or 5 individual molds.

Refrigerate 4 hours or until firm. Unmold. Serve with crisp salad greens and salad dressing, if desired.

Makes 5 servings.

Note: Recipe can be doubled, using 5-cup mold.

THREE-FRUIT MOLD

1 cup boiling water
1 package
(4-serving size)
Jell-O brand
gelatin, any
flavor
1 can (8 ounces)
crushed
pineapple
Cold water
1 tablespoon
lemon juice
1¼ cups diced
grapefruit and
orange sections

Stir boiling water into gelatin in medium bowl 2 minutes or until completely dissolved.

Drain pineapple, reserving liquid. Add water to reserved liquid to make ¾ cup. Stir measured liquids and lemon juice into gelatin. Refrigerate 1½ hours or until thickened. Stir in fruit. Pour into 4-cup mold.

Refrigerate 4 hours or until firm. Unmold. Serve with crisp salad greens and salad dressing, if desired.

Makes 6 servings.

SEAFOOD MOLD

¾ cup boiling water
1 package (4-serving size) Jell-O brand lemon flavor gelatin
1 tablespoon dry mustard
1½ teaspoons seafood seasoning
2 cups chopped cooked seafood*
½ cup chopped celery
½ cup chopped green onions
½ cup chopped red pepper
½ cup Miracle Whip salad dressing
2 tablespoons lemon juice

Use scallops, shrimp, crabmeat or combination.

Stir boiling water into gelatin, mustard and seasoning in large bowl 2 minutes or until gelatin is completely dissolved. Stir in remaining ingredients; mix well. Spoon into 3-cup mold or bowl.

Refrigerate 3 hours or until firm. Unmold onto serving platter. Garnish with crisp salad greens.

Makes 6 servings.
Kym Dierde Gibson
Executive Chef
The Blair House
Washington, DC

MY MOTHER GWENDOLYN OLIVIA CRAIG SAID...

"The road of life will be of your own choosing. Through dedication your goals will be obtainable; through hard work and education your possibilities will abound."

Deidre Kym Gibson
Washington, DC

SOUTHERN TURKEY SALAD

2 cups Miracle Whip salad dressing, divided
½ cup sweet pickle relish
½ teaspoon salt
¼ teaspoon pepper
4 cups chopped cooked turkey breast
2 stalks celery, chopped
3 hard-cooked eggs, chopped
½ cup chopped green pepper
1 jar (4 ounces) sliced pimientos, drained
Lettuce and crackers

Stir salad dressing, relish, salt and pepper in small bowl. Mix turkey, celery, eggs, green pepper and pimientos in large bowl. Add salad dressing mixture; toss to coat. Cover.

Refrigerate at least 1 hour. Stir in additional salad dressing, if desired. Serve on lettuce leaves with crackers.

Makes 12 servings.

TASTY CHICKEN SALAD

8 boneless, skinless chicken breast halves, cooked, cut into chunks
2 cups coarsely chopped walnuts
1 small red onion, diced
1 cup Miracle Whip salad dressing
½ teaspoon salt
¼ teaspoon ground red pepper
1 can (11 ounces) Mandarin orange segments, drained

Mix chicken, walnuts, onion, salad dressing, salt and pepper in large bowl; cover.

Refrigerate at least 1 hour or until ready to serve. Stir in additional salad dressing, if desired. Garnish with orange segments.

Makes 8 servings.

CAROLINA TUNA MACARONI SALAD

1 package (7¼ ounces) Kraft macaroni & cheese dinner
1 can (6⅛ ounces) tuna, drained, flaked
3 hard-cooked eggs, chopped
¾ cup Kraft sandwich spread
1 small green pepper, chopped
1 small onion, finely chopped
½ teaspoon pepper
¼ teaspoon salt

Prepare dinner as directed on package. Add remaining ingredients; mix well.

Refrigerate until ready to serve. Add additional sandwich spread before serving, if desired.

Makes 6 servings.

MY MOTHER MARY FRANCES LEWIS BETSCH SAID...

"In my eyes, my Mother was bigger than life. She was 'regular folks' and yet she was always reachable, there for me. To this very day she's still with me. When this marvelous Mom of mine spoke, I believed whatever she said and stretched to catch whatever rainbow she assured me was within my grasp. That said, you will understand my Mother's advice to me as I cried in response to something my grandfather said. Laughing at my announcement that I wanted to be an anthropoligist, my grandfather seriously asked: 'How will you ever make a living doing that?' I can still hear Mary Frances Lewis Betsch's words as she comforted me: 'If you do work that you hate, you will be miserable for the rest of your life. Find work that you love. If this is your passion, follow it. But whatever you do as your life's work, you must do it well!' And that's the advice I give to my 2000 surrogate daughters at Spelman College."

Dr. Johnnetta B. Cole
President of Spelman College

MY MOTHER BERNICE MCMURRY SCOTT SAID...

*W*hen I first remember my mother, she must have been in her early 20's. I can still see her cooking breakfast on a large, wood-burning stove in our kitchen in the small frame house on my grandfather's farm. I see her drawing water from the well in our back yard, never complaining, because many of our neighbors had to go to the stream. On Sundays she was an impressive figure in church where she played the piano. Mother had only a fourth grade education which she got by going to school three months a year. She 'minded' cows, worked in the fields, married at 16 and began having children. She used to say, 'I have never been a child; I've been a woman all my life.' Despite her life and education, she had a good mind and practical wisdom. She seemed more resentful of the injustices of racism than my Father, who said people are bad because conditions make them that way.

The day came when I went to my mother with the question every black child sooner or later asks parents, 'Why?' My mother answered in much the same way black mothers have for generations. 'You are just as good as anyone else,' she said. 'You get an education and try to be somebody. Then you won't have to be kicked around by anybody, and you won't have to depend on anyone for your livelihood.' I remember these words every Mother's Day, and I know that they are being repeated in thousands of black households across the country."

Coretta Scott King
Founding President/CEO
The Martin Luther King, Jr. Center
for Nonviolent Social Change

BISCUITS

Hot bread is a must on African-American tables. At breakfast, the bread is usually a biscuit. Ranging from fluffy and flaky to substantial and suitable for sopping, biscuits come in all sizes and shapes. They appear split and slathered with butter and syrup at the breakfast table, jazzed up with the addition of sweet potatoes or pumpkin at dinner, or split with a slice of country ham and a dab of mustard as a snack or a fancy hors d'oeuvre.

Light-as-air baking powder biscuits are the queens of many African-American tables. However, the undisputed empress of the biscuit world is the silky-textured, beaten biscuit which is prepared after the dough has been pounded steadily with a mallet.

Today, biscuits are no longer a breakfast necessity but more often a weekend or holiday treat. No matter what time of day that they're served, when they emerge from the oven lightly browned and hot, we're all transported back to the Saturday breakfasts of long ago, when folks gathered around the table to sop syrup and scarf down those wonderful delicacies known as biscuits.

—Jessica B. Harris

SHORTCAKE BISCUITS

1¾ **cups flour**
4 **teaspoons baking powder**
1 **teaspoon sugar**
½ **teaspoon salt**
½ **teaspoon cream of tartar**
½ **cup (1 stick) margarine or butter**
⅔ **cup milk**

Heat oven to 450°F.

Mix flour, baking powder, sugar, salt and cream of tartar in large bowl. Cut in margarine until mixture resembles coarse crumbs. Add milk to flour mixture; stir until soft dough forms.

Knead dough on lightly floured surface until smooth. Pat or roll lightly until dough is ½ inch thick. Cut with floured 2-inch cookie cutter. Place on ungreased cookie sheet.

Bake 10 to 12 minutes or until golden brown.

Makes 14.

BAKING POWDER BISCUITS

1¾ **cups flour**
1 **tablespoon baking powder**
½ **teaspoon salt**
⅓ **cup shortening or margarine**
¾ **cup milk**

Heat oven to 450°F.

Mix flour, baking powder and salt in large bowl. Cut in margarine until mixture resembles coarse crumbs. Add milk to flour mixture; stir until soft dough forms.

Knead dough on lightly floured surface until smooth. Pat or roll lightly until dough is ½ inch thick. Cut with floured 2-inch cookie cutter. Place on ungreased cookie sheet.

Bake 10 minutes or until golden brown.

Makes 16.

Drop Biscuits: Prepare as directed, dropping dough by table-spoonfuls onto ungreased cookie sheet. *Makes 16.*

Skillet Biscuits: Prepare as directed, patting or rolling dough lightly until ¼ inch thick. Cut with floured 2-inch cookie cutter. Heat large skillet 1 minute on low heat. Place biscuits in skillet; cover. Cook 14 minutes or until brown, turning once. *Makes 16.*

Biscuit Doughnuts: Prepare as directed, patting or rolling dough lightly until ¼ inch thick. Cut with floured 2-inch cookie cutter. Add oil to large skillet to depth of 1 inch; heat on medium heat to 400°F. Add biscuits; cook 5 minutes or until browned, turning once. Drain on paper towels. Sprinkle with sugar, if desired. *Makes 12.*

Buttermilk Biscuits: Prepare as directed, substituting buttermilk for the milk and adding ¼ teaspoon baking powder to flour mixture. *Makes 16.*

MY MOTHER OLA FALLEN-HAILEY SAID...

"The race was not won by the swift or the strong but the one who holds on and proves herself faithful."

Carolyn Hailey Grey
Billerica, MA

MOTHER'S SWEET CORNMEAL BUNS

1½ cups flour
2 teaspoons baking powder
1 cup yellow cornmeal
¼ cup half-and-half
¼ cup milk
2 teaspoons grated lemon peel
½ teaspoon vanilla
⅓ cup margarine or butter, softened
¾ cup sugar, divided
2 tablespoons honey
1 egg
  Powdered sugar

Heat oven to 375°F. Grease cookie sheet.

Mix flour, baking powder and cornmeal in small bowl.

Stir half-and-half, milk, peel and vanilla in another small bowl.

Beat margarine, ½ cup of the sugar and honey in large bowl with electric mixer on medium speed until light and fluffy. Add egg; beat well. Add flour mixture alternately with half-and-half mixture, beating after each addition until smooth.

Knead dough on lightly floured surface until smooth. Divide into 12 pieces. Shape into balls; flatten each ball until ¾ inch thick. Brush tops with water; sprinkle with remaining ¼ cup sugar. Place on greased cookie sheet, sugar side up.

Bake 15 minutes or until golden brown. Remove from pan. Cool on wire rack. Sprinkle with powdered sugar.

Makes 12.

MY MOTHER RUBY KIRKLAND SAID...

"To err is human. To forgive is divine."

Pamela Kirkland
Washington, DC

CORN BREAD

Fluffy yellow corn bread straight from the oven, piping hot and ready to be split open for a waiting pat of butter…it's the traditional accompaniment to many a meal. Somehow the taste of hot corn bread just seems to blend perfectly with the smokey taste of country hams. Nothing sops up gravy or soaks up the pot likker from a mess of greens as well. It's the first item that disappears from the bread basket at any soul food restaurant.

As much a part of African-American life as family reunions and summer barbecues, corn bread is also a part of our history. It was essential to our survival as a people as well.

During the tribulations of slavery, individuals received rations of cornmeal, which was the staff of life for many. The cornmeal was transformed into various dishes from corn pones to hoecakes to hush puppies and mushes, to our all time favorite — corn bread.

In much of the South, the cornmeal that goes into the corn bread is white. In the North and in other areas of the country, it's yellow. The best is stone-ground, and some is even self-rising. Whatever color the cornmeal is — yellow or white, whatever the shape — whether baked in squares or corn sticks or even in muffin shapes, corn bread is a piece of our history on the table.

—Jessica B. Harris

SOUTHERN-STYLE CORN BREAD

1 **cup flour**
1 **cup white or yellow cornmeal**
2 **tablespoons sugar**
2 **teaspoons baking powder**
1 **teaspoon baking soda**
1 **teaspoon salt**
2 **eggs**
1½ **cups buttermilk**
⅓ **cup shortening or butter, melted**

Heat oven to 425°F. Grease 9-inch square baking pan.

Mix flour, cornmeal, sugar, baking powder, baking soda and salt in large bowl. Beat eggs in medium bowl; stir in buttermilk and shortening. Add to flour mixture. Stir just until moistened. Pour into prepared pan.

Bake 25 minutes or until golden brown.

Makes 10 servings.

HERITAGE RECIPE

HOECAKE

1 cup cornmeal
½ teaspoon salt
1 cup boiling water
2 tablespoons oil

Mix cornmeal and salt in medium bowl. Stir in water; mix well.

Heat oil in 8-inch cast iron skillet. Spread dough in skillet; flatten with spoon. Cook 1 to 2 minutes on each side or until browned.

Makes 4 servings.

HERITAGE RECIPE

SPOON BREAD

1 cup cornmeal
1 tablespoon sugar
1 teaspoon baking powder
1 teaspoon salt
1 cup milk
¼ cup (½ stick) margarine or butter
3 eggs, separated

Heat oven to 350°F. Grease 1½-quart casserole.

Mix cornmeal, sugar, baking powder and salt in medium saucepan. Stir in milk. Cook until mixture is thickened and smooth. Remove from heat. Stir in margarine and slightly beaten egg yolks.

Beat egg whites in medium bowl with electric mixer on high speed until stiff peaks form. Gently stir into cornmeal mixture. Pour into prepared casserole.

Bake 35 minutes or until golden.

Makes 8 servings.

HERITAGE RECIPE

HUSH PUPPIES

1 **cup cornmeal**
1 **teaspoon baking powder**
¾ **teaspoon sugar**
½ **teaspoon salt**
1 **egg**
½ **cup milk**
2 **tablespoons shortening, melted**
2 **cups oil**

Mix cornmeal, baking powder, sugar and salt in large bowl.

Beat egg in small bowl; stir in milk and shortening. Add to cornmeal mixture; stir just until moistened.

Heat oil in large heavy saucepan. Drop cornmeal mixture by table-spoonfuls into hot oil; cook until golden, turning to brown evenly.

Makes 12.

HERITAGE RECIPE

STUFFING HUSH PUPPIES

1½ **cups Stove Top cornbread stuffing mix in the canister**
¾ **cup flour**
2 **teaspoons baking powder**
1 **egg**
¾ **cup milk**
2 **tablespoons Parkay spread stick, melted**
3 **cups oil**

Mix stuffing mix, flour and baking powder in medium bowl. Beat egg in small bowl; stir in milk and spread. Add to stuffing mix mixture; stir just until moistened. Let stand 5 minutes.

Heat oil in large skillet on medium heat to 350°F. Carefully add table-spoonfuls of batter, a few at a time; cook 3 minutes or until golden brown, turning once. Drain on paper towels; keep warm. Reheat oil to 350°F between batches. Serve warm.

Makes 2 dozen.

MY MOTHER ISABELL LOIS "IZZIE" WILLIAMS SAID...

"Education is very important but don't become an educated fool."

Willie B. Kennedy
San Francisco, CA

CREAMED CORN BREAD

2 cups Stove Top cornbread stuffing mix in the canister
1 cup flour
¼ cup sugar
4 teaspoons baking powder
1 can (8 ounces) cream-style corn
½ cup milk
¼ cup (½ stick) margarine or butter, melted
1 egg, slightly beaten

Heat oven to 450°F. Grease 9-inch square baking pan.

Mix stuffing mix, flour, sugar and baking powder in large bowl. Stir in corn, milk, margarine and egg. Pour into prepared pan.

Bake 20 minutes or until golden. Cut into squares. Serve warm.

Makes 16.

Creamed Corn Sticks: Prepare as directed, greasing cast-iron corn stick mold. Heating oven to 450°F. Place prepared mold in oven; heat 10 minutes. Spoon ¼ cup batter into each indentation of mold. Bake 12 minutes or until golden.

Makes 16.

MY MOTHER MARGURITE "MARGIE" MORRIS WATTS SAID...

"Never Proceed to eat in front of an unexpected guest when there is not enough food to go around. If you insisted on eating in their presence, then it was customary to invite them unconditionally to eat and to share. With this in mind, i always prepare enough to share."

Barbara Watts Maxwell
Edison, NJ

BLACK EYE PEA FRITTERS

This is not a Mother memory, but rather a memory of my father. My father didn't believe in throwing away anything. One night, when we didn't eat all of the black eye peas, he said, "Don't worry, you'll see them again." The next morning, when we came downstairs, we smelled the most delicious thing cooking, and it was fritters. We ate them all, and then father said, "Those were the black eye peas you left last night." They were wonderful. My father believed that "waste not, want not" was the best way.

Angeline Newberry Donaldson
Newberry, South Carolina

BLACK EYE PEA FRITTERS

2 **cups pancake mix**
1 **cup cooked black eye peas**
Log Cabin syrup or dark molasses

Prepare pancake mix as directed on package. Stir in peas.

Using about ¼ cup batter for each fritter, cook on hot greased griddle until bubbles form on top. Turn to brown on other side. Serve warm with syrup or molasses.

Makes 20.

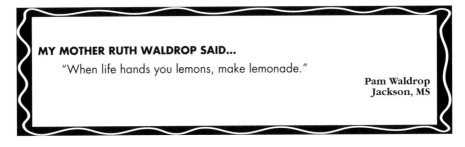

MY MOTHER RUTH WALDROP SAID...
"When life hands you lemons, make lemonade."

Pam Waldrop
Jackson, MS

♡ A FEW BEANS OR GRAINS OF RICE INSIDE A SALT SHAKER WILL KEEP IT FLOWING FREELY EVEN IN THE DAMPEST WEATHER.

CORN FRITTERS

½ cup flour
1 teaspoon salt
¾ teaspoon baking powder
⅛ teaspoon pepper
2 eggs
3 tablespoons milk
1¾ cups frozen whole kernel corn, thawed
2 tablespoons Parkay spread stick, melted
2½ cups oil
Log Cabin syrup

Mix flour, salt, baking powder and pepper in large bowl. Beat eggs in small bowl; stir in milk. Add to flour mixture; stir just until moistened. Toss corn with spread in small bowl. Stir into batter.

Heat oil in large skillet on medium heat to 350°F. Carefully add table-spoonfuls of batter, a few at a time; cook about 5 minutes or until golden brown, turning once. Drain on paper towels; keep warm. Reheat oil to 350°F between batches. Serve warm with syrup.

Makes 12.

Deviled Ham Corn Fritters: Prepare as directed, omitting milk and ½ teaspoon of the salt. Add 1 can (4½ ounces) deviled ham with the corn.

FRUIT FRITTERS

1 cup pancake mix
¼ teaspoon ground cinnamon
1 egg
½ cup milk
1 cup diced peeled apple or mashed ripe banana
2½ cups oil
Log Cabin syrup

Mix pancake mix and cinnamon in large bowl. Beat egg in small bowl; stir in milk. Add to pancake mix mixture; stir just until moistened. Stir in fruit.

Heat oil in large skillet on medium heat to 350°F. Carefully add table-spoonfuls of batter, a few at a time; cook 3 minutes or until golden brown, turning once. Drain on paper towels; keep warm. Reheat oil to 350°F between batches. Serve warm with syrup.

Makes 14.

MAPLEY CARROT MUFFINS

2 cups flour
1 cup sugar
2 teaspoons baking soda
2 teaspoons ground cinnamon
½ teaspoon salt
⅛ teaspoon ground allspice
⅛ teaspoon ground nutmeg
3 eggs
¾ cup Log Cabin syrup
¾ cup oil
1 can (8 ounces) crushed pineapple, drained
2½ cups shredded carrots
⅔ cup chopped walnuts

Heat oven to 350°F. Grease or line muffin pans with paper bake cups.

Mix flour, sugar, baking soda, cinnamon, salt, allspice and nutmeg in large bowl. Beat eggs in medium bowl; stir in syrup and oil. Add to flour mixture; stir just until moistened. Stir in pineapple, carrots and walnuts. Spoon batter into prepared pans, filling each cup ¾ full.

Bake 20 to 25 minutes or until toothpick inserted in center of muffin comes out clean. Serve warm.

Makes 24.

MY MOTHER JESSE MAE "MA DEAR" HARRIS SAID...

When confronted with seemingly insurmountable situations: "Let go and let God. It's difficult to see the picture when you are in the frame."

Vern Goff
Washington, DC

MAPLEY PECAN MUFFINS

2 cups flour
¼ cup firmly packed brown sugar
1½ teaspoons baking powder
¼ teaspoon salt
1 egg
½ cup Log Cabin syrup
½ cup milk
⅓ cup margarine or butter, melted
1 teaspoon vanilla
1 cup chopped pecans
1 tablespoon sugar
½ teaspoon ground cinnamon

Heat oven to 400°F. Grease or line muffin pan with paper bake cups.

Mix flour, brown sugar, baking powder and salt in large bowl. Beat egg in small bowl; stir in syrup, milk, margarine and vanilla. Add to flour mixture; stir just until moistened. (Batter will be lumpy.) Stir in pecans. Spoon batter into prepared pan, filling each cup ⅔ full.

Mix sugar and cinnamon in small cup. Sprinkle evenly over each muffin.

Bake 15 to 20 minutes or until golden brown. Serve warm.

Makes 12.

SOUTHERN FLAPJACKS

1 cup flour
¼ cup yellow cornmeal
1 tablespoon sugar
1½ teaspoons baking powder
½ teaspoon salt
1 egg, beaten
1¼ cups milk
2 tablespoons oil

Stir flour, cornmeal, sugar, baking powder and salt in medium bowl. Stir in egg. Stir in milk and oil.

Using about ¼ cup batter for each flapjack, cook on hot greased griddle until bubbles form on top. Turn to brown on other side.

Makes about 8 (4-inch) flapjacks.

MY MOTHER FLORA B. NAPIER SAID...

"If you have a friend, keep her so but let her not your secrets know. For if your friend becomes your foe, all the world your secrets will know."

Esther Napier Alli
Patterson, NJ

ZUCCHINI BREAD

3 cups flour
4 teaspoons baking powder
1 tablespoon ground cinnamon
1 teaspoon baking soda
1 teaspoon salt
3 eggs
2 cups sugar
1 cup oil
2 cups shredded zucchini
1 tablespoon vanilla
½ cup chopped nuts

Heat oven to 350°F. Grease 2 (8x4-inch) loaf pans.

Stir flour, baking powder, cinnamon, baking soda and salt in medium bowl. Beat eggs in large bowl. Mix in sugar, oil and vanilla. Stir in zucchini. Add flour mixture; stir just until moistened. Stir in nuts. Pour into prepared pans.

Bake 60 minutes or until toothpick inserted in center comes out clean. Cool 10 minutes; remove from pans. Cool completely on wire rack.

Makes 2 loaves.

RAISIN SPICE OATMEAL BREAD

1½ cups flour
1½ teaspoons salt
1 teaspoon baking soda
1 teaspoon baking powder
1 teaspoon ground cinnamon
½ teaspoon ground nutmeg
2 eggs
1 cup applesauce
⅔ cup firmly packed brown sugar
⅓ cup oil
1 cup quick-cooking oats
1 cup raisins
½ cup chopped nuts (optional)

Heat oven to 350°F. Grease 9x5-inch loaf pan.

Stir flour, salt, baking soda, baking powder, cinnamon and nutmeg in large bowl. Beat eggs in medium bowl. Mix in applesauce, sugar and oil. Add to flour mixture; stir just until moistened. Stir in oats, raisins and nuts. Pour into prepared pan.

Bake 50 to 60 minutes or until toothpick inserted in center comes out clean. Cool 10 minutes; remove from pan. Cool completely on wire rack.

Makes 1 loaf.

SWEET POTATO NUT BREAD

3½ cups flour
1 tablespoon baking powder
1½ teaspoons baking soda
½ teaspoon ground cloves
½ teaspoon salt
4 eggs
2½ cups sugar
⅔ cup oil
1 can (16 ounces) sweet potatoes, drained, mashed
⅔ cup water
1 cup chopped pecans

Heat oven to 350°F. Grease 2 (8x4-inch) loaf pans.

Stir flour, baking powder, baking soda, cloves and salt in medium bowl. Beat eggs in large bowl. Mix in sugar and oil. Stir in sweet potatoes and water. Add flour mixture; stir just until moistened. Stir in nuts. Pour into prepared pans.

Bake 50 minutes or until toothpick inserted in center comes out clean. Cool 10 minutes; remove from pans. Cool completely on wire rack.

Makes 2 loaves.

PUMPKIN BREAD

3 cups flour
1 cup firmly packed brown sugar
2 teaspoons baking soda
1 teaspoon ground cinnamon
½ teaspoon ground cloves
½ teaspoon ground nutmeg
½ teaspoon salt
3 eggs
1 can (16 ounces) pumpkin
¾ cup Log Cabin syrup
⅔ cup oil
1 cup chopped walnuts
1 cup raisins

Heat oven to 350°F. Grease 2 (9x5-inch) loaf pans.

Mix flour, sugar, baking soda, cinnamon, cloves, nutmeg and salt in large bowl. Beat eggs in medium bowl; stir in pumpkin, syrup and oil. Add to flour mixture; stir just until moistened. (Batter will be lumpy.) Stir in nuts and raisins. Pour into prepared pans.

Bake 50 to 60 minutes or until toothpick inserted in center comes out clean. Cool 10 minutes; remove from pans. Cool completely on wire rack.

Makes 2 loaves.

BANANA CHOCOLATE CHIP BREAD

2 cups flour
½ cup firmly packed brown sugar
2 teaspoons baking powder
¼ teaspoon salt
2 eggs
2 small ripe bananas, mashed (about 1 cup)
½ cup Log Cabin syrup
⅓ cup vegetable oil
¼ cup milk
1 cup Baker's semi-sweet real chocolate chips*
½ cup chopped nuts

*Or use 1 package (4 ounces) Baker's German sweet chocolate, coarsely chopped.

Heat oven to 350°F. Grease 9x5-inch loaf pan.

Mix flour, sugar, baking powder and salt in large bowl. Beat eggs in small bowl; stir in bananas, syrup, oil and milk. Add to flour mixture; stir just until moistened. (Batter will be lumpy.) Stir in chocolate chips and nuts. Pour into prepared pan.

Bake 60 to 65 minutes or until toothpick inserted in center comes out clean. Cool 10 minutes; remove from pan. Cool completely on wire rack.

Makes 1 loaf.

EASY STICKY BUNS

½ cup Log Cabin syrup
¼ cup (½ stick) margarine or butter
½ cup chopped pecans
1½ teaspoons ground cinnamon
1 can (7½ ounces) refrigerated biscuits

Heat oven to 450°F.

Bring syrup and margarine to boil in small saucepan; cook and stir 2 minutes. Add nuts and cinnamon; cook 1 minute. Pour into 8-inch round baking pan. Arrange biscuits in pan.

Bake 8 to 10 minutes or until golden brown. Invert immediately onto serving plate. Serve warm.

Makes 10.

MY MOTHER BERTHA "CHUBBY" HOLTE SAID...

"I was the original 'Mama's girl' — talk about tied to her apron strings, I was like her shadow, following her everywhere, always underfoot as she went about the kitchen doing her cooking, cleaning and ironing. Everything I thought was good in the world was right there — my Mother, the sparkling counter tops, the smell of food cooking on the stove — but my Mother knew better, she knew I was hiding out from the world.

You see I was so-o-o-o-o-o shy and timid I'd make excuses to stay there with her in the kitchen. When she'd get too busy to do anything more than 'uh huh' me, I'd dress up my cat for extra company and have little parties. I didn't have many friends except my Mother and sisters, but Mama knew I couldn't go through life like that. She'd try anything to get me to join the other kids outside and get so exasperated when all her attempts failed. One day, knowing I was saving for something special, she promised me a quarter if I would just go outside and make friends with the neighbor's children.

I found out real fast that the reward was worth a lot more than 25 cents. There was a whole world open to me — a world filled with warm and loving folks just outside my kitchen door. Years later I figured my Mother knew that she couldn't always be there for me so she helped me face the world on my own."

Patti LaBelle
Queen of Rock 'n Soul

POTATO ROLLS

Potato rolls are a family favorite. We serve them for all special holidays and family functions when we're eating at home. If we don't have potato rolls, somebody's sure to ask for them and comment on it. The rolls originated with my grandmother Rita, and she passed the recipe on to my Mother, Lillian, who passed it on to me. I cook them and my daughter cooks them, too, and I take them to my son's for family gatherings. This Christmas, I'm starting my ten-year-old granddaughter with the recipe. Potato Rolls take a lot of time, but they're worth the bother because they're delicious.

Diane Butler
West Covina, California

RITA'S POTATO ROLLS

1 **package active dry yeast**
¼ **cup warm water (105° to 115°F)**
1 **cup mashed potatoes**
¾ **cup shortening**
¾ **cup sugar**
1 **cup milk**
1 **teaspoon salt**
2 **eggs, beaten**
5 **cups flour, divided**

Sprinkle yeast over warm water in small bowl; stir until dissolved. Let stand 5 minutes.

Place potatoes, shortening and sugar in large bowl. Bring milk just to boil in small saucepan. Gradually stir hot milk into potato mixture. Stir in salt, eggs and yeast mixture. Stir in 1 cup of the flour until well blended. Gradually stir in remaining 4 cups flour until dough forms.

Knead dough on lightly floured surface about 10 minutes or until smooth and elastic. Add additional flour if dough is too moist. Place in large greased bowl; turn dough over so that top is greased. Cover with towel. Let rise in warm place about 1 hour or until doubled. Punch dough down; knead on lightly floured surface.

Pat dough into rectangle. Cut into 24 pieces. Shape into rounds. Place on greased 15x10x1-inch baking pan. Cover with towel. Let rise in warm place about 45 minutes or until doubled. Meanwhile, heat oven to 400°F.

Bake 20 to 25 minutes or until golden brown.

Makes 24.

MY MOTHER CORINNE "LACY" LONG SAID...

"You've got to wear this world like a loose cloak."

Marlene A. Harris
Atlanta, GA

DINNER ROLLS

¾ **cup hot water (140° to 160°F)**
½ **cup sugar**
1 **tablespoon salt**
¼ **cup shortening**
2 **packages active dry yeast**
1 **cup warm water (105° to 115°F)**
1 **egg, beaten**
5 **cups sifted flour Melted margarine or butter**

Stir hot water, sugar, salt and shortening in small bowl; cool until lukewarm.

Meanwhile, sprinkle yeast over warm water in large bowl; stir until dissolved. Let stand 5 minutes. Stir in sugar mixture. Add egg and 2½ cups of the flour; beat until well blended. Gradually stir in remaining 2½ cups flour; beat 1 minute, using a wooden spoon, or until dough pulls away from side of bowl and forms a ball. Add additional flour if dough is too sticky. Dough will be soft.

Place dough in large greased bowl; turn dough over so that top is greased. Cover with plastic wrap. Let rise in warm place about 1½ hours or until doubled. Punch dough down.

Divide dough in half. Shape each half into 16-inch log. Cut each log into 16 pieces. Roll into smooth balls. Place ⅓ inch apart on 2 greased 8-inch square baking pans. Cover with plastic wrap. Let rise in warm place about 1 hour or until doubled. Meanwhile, heat oven to 375°F. Brush with margarine.

Bake 20 minutes or until golden brown.

Makes 32.

 A FRESH BAY LEAF INSIDE YOUR FLOUR CANISTER WILL KEEP THE BUGS AWAY.

CATHERINE'S COUNTRY ROLLS

2 **packages active dry yeast***
¼ **cup warm water (105° to 115°F)***
2 **cups milk**
2 **eggs, separated**
2 **tablespoons sugar**
1 **teaspoon salt**
6 **cups flour**
5 **tablespoons oil**
  Melted butter

Or use 1 yeast cake and omit water.

Sprinkle yeast over warm water in large bowl; stir until dissolved. Let stand 5 minutes.

Add milk, egg yolks, sugar and salt; mix thoroughly. Stir in flour until sticky dough forms. Beat egg whites in small bowl until foamy. Stir into flour mixture. Stir in oil. Add additional flour if dough is too sticky.

Place dough in large greased bowl; turn dough over so that top is greased. Cover with towel. Let rise in warm place about 1 hour or until doubled. Knead dough on lightly floured surface.

Roll dough to ½ inch thick. Cut with floured 2-inch biscuit cutter. Brush with melted butter. Fold roll over like a sheet of paper to make parkay shape. Place in greased 13x9-inch pan.

Heat oven to 375°F. Bake 15 to 20 minutes or until golden brown. Remove from oven. Brush with additional melted butter.

Makes 26.
Camille O. Cosby

MY MOTHER CATHERINE C. HANKS SAID...

"My Mother's maternal grandparents were landowners in Virginia. To own land, grow our food, build our home and enjoy nature was the wisdom my Mother passed on to me as part of her special family legacy. This message, like my great-grandparents' farm, continues to pass from one generation to the next."

Dr. Camille O. Cosby
Educator and Philanthropist

MY MOTHER PROTEONE MARIE MALVEAUX SAID...

*M*y Mother is a social worker by profession, but an artist by inclination. She painted her kitchen powder blue and white, with affirmations, prayers, and pictures of fruit lovingly accenting her walls. Her kitchen is this pungent personal space where smells of beans and rice combine with the lingering odor of Dixie Peach applied to new-pressed hair. I remember sitting at the window with my typewriter, musing with my fingers, caught up in the smells, images and sounds. Proteone Marie Malveaux has made her kitchen a magnet pulling us into her personal space, a place where one can learn her, love her, love oneself.

Hot food, hard work and hugs were my Mother's prescriptions for any problem. My first semester home from college, I worried that I'd not hit my goal of a "B+" average. "Have some soup," Mommy said, ladling a vegetable and pasta-rich broth into my bowl. Even now, I can see the steam rising from the pot, and can smell the aromatic mix of garlic, thyme and rosemary. "Did you try?" she asked, as she dished up her own bowl and sat across from me. Her face could not have been closer to mine if I had mashed my image into a mirror. Her eyes were intense, but also accepting. the smells were a blanket that embraced me. Even before I put a spoon to my lips, I felt better.

"If you did your best, it will work out," she said and opened up her arms so that I could be held and reassured. A few days later, the grades came in. I didn't hit that "B+" average my first semester, just a B. The killer was a "C+" in history, dragging down my GPA. Something simultaneously stern and loving was said over juice the next day. "How was the first semester?" a relative said, as platters were passed around. "Julianne did an outstanding job, but next time she'll do better at history." The "C" was never mentioned again, and for the rest of my winter sojourn home, my first semester was discussed with such pride that I thought I'd earned all "A's."

Pass or fail, I'd rather do it in the kitchen than in the living room, library or bedroom. Smells, sounds and attitudes were such, in the kitchen, that they cut life's edge. My Mother's kitchen remains a place full of love, life and the unspoken assurance that hot food, hard work and hugs make life a sweeter and more satisfying place than it might be. Whether I hit the mark or miss a little, I know my Mother's kitchen is a reassuring place. Hot food, hard work, and hugs….What else could a woman possibly need to take an upside down world and set it right?

Dr. Julianne Malveaux
Economist and Syndicated Columnist

CELEBRATING OUR MOTHERS' MAIN DISHES

AUNT MATTIE'S BAKED CHICKEN

2 pounds skinless chicken pieces
2 tablespoons soy sauce
2 tablespoons Worcestershire sauce
4 teaspoons lemon juice
1 teaspoon lemon pepper
1 teaspoon poultry seasoning
1 green pepper, chopped
1 small onion, chopped

Place chicken in 12x8-inch baking dish.

Stir soy sauce, Worcestershire, lemon juice, lemon pepper and poultry seasoning in small bowl. Pour over chicken; cover. Refrigerate 30 minutes.

Heat oven to 350°F.

Top chicken with pepper and onion; cover.

Bake 1 hour or until chicken is cooked through.

Makes 4 servings.

BAKED CHICKEN WINGS

16 chicken wings, separated at joints, tips discarded
½ cup water
½ teaspoon salt
¼ teaspoon pepper
6 slices Oscar Mayer bacon
1 medium onion, chopped
1 small green pepper, chopped

Heat oven to 350°F.

Arrange chicken in single layer in 10x15-inch baking pan. Add water; sprinkle with salt and pepper. Top with bacon.

Bake 30 minutes. Turn chicken over; add green pepper and onions. Bake 30 minutes or until cooked through.

Makes 4 servings.

Crispy Chicken Wings: Prepare as directed, baking 30 minutes. Remove chicken from oven. Heat broiler. Broil 15 minutes, turning occasionally.

MY MOTHER INEZ H. MCCULLOUGH SAID...

"When your Father and I are not reachable, just pray."

Janie S. McCullough
Silver Spring, MD

TURKEY PEPPER À LA KING

2 **tablespoons margarine or butter**
1 **each green, red and yellow pepper, chopped**
2 **tablespoons flour**
2 **teaspoons salt**
½ **teaspoon pepper**
1 **quart half-and-half or milk**
4 **cups chopped cooked turkey breast**
   Hot cooked rice

Melt margarine in large skillet on medium heat. Add peppers; cook and stir until tender. Stir in flour, salt and pepper. Add half-and-half; bring to boil. Reduce heat and simmer until sauce begins to thicken. Add turkey and simmer over low heat 15 minutes. Serve over rice. Sprinkle with paprika, if desired.

Makes 6 servings.

SPICED CHICKEN

1 **tablespoon oil**
1 **teaspoon chili powder**
1 **teaspoon curry powder**
1 **clove garlic, minced**
1 **container (8 ounces) plain yogurt**
1 **teaspoon ground cinnamon**
1 **teaspoon coriander seed, crushed**
1 **teaspoon honey**
½ **teaspoon celery salt**
½ **teaspoon salt**
2 **broiler-fryer chickens, cut up (2 to 2½ pounds each)**

Heat oil in small saucepan on medium heat. Add chili powder, curry powder and garlic; cook 1 minute. Cool.

Stir yogurt, cinnamon, coriander seed, honey, celery salt, salt and chili powder mixture in small bowl.

Place chicken in shallow dish; pierce with fork in several places. Pour yogurt mixture over chicken, turning to coat; cover. Refrigerate 20 minutes.

Heat broiler. Place chicken on rack of broiler pan. Broil 5 inches from heat, turning often, 30 to 40 minutes or until cooked through.

Makes 8 servings.

CHICKEN WITH TOMATOES & GREEN CHILIES

12 ounces spaghetti, uncooked, broken into pieces
4 tablespoons Parkay Spread stick or butter
1 medium onion, chopped
1 small green pepper, chopped
1 pound Velveeta pasteurized process cheese spread, cubed
1 can (10 ounces) whole tomatoes and green chilies, undrained, cut up
½ cup milk
1 tablespoon Worcestershire sauce
5 cups diced cooked chicken

Prepare spaghetti as directed on package; drain.

Melt spread in large skillet on medium-high heat. Add onion and pepper; cook and stir until tender. Add Velveeta pasteurized process cheese spread, tomatoes, milk and Worcestershire; cook and stir on medium heat until sauce is smooth. Stir in chicken.

Heat oven to 350°F.

Place ½ of the spaghetti in 4-quart casserole. Top with ½ of the chicken mixture. Repeat layers. Stir gently to mix; cover.

Bake 45 to 60 minutes or until bubbly, stirring occasionally.

Makes 10 servings.

MY MOTHER MOZELLE REED SAID...

"It is not important if you love a man but very important that he loves you. For if he does, he will treat you very well and take good care of you and then you can't help but love him in return."

Marci Scott
Syracuse, NY

QUICK CHICKEN JAMBALAYA

1 tablespoon oil
¼ pound andouille or other smoked sausage, sliced
2 boneless skinless chicken breasts, cut into cubes
1 medium onion, chopped
1 small green pepper, cut into strips
1 stalk celery, sliced
1 clove garlic, minced
1 can (14½ ounces) Cajun-style stewed tomatoes
1 package (10 ounces) frozen cut okra
1 can (8 ounces) tomato sauce
2 teaspoons Creole seasoning
1½ cups Minute original or premium rice, uncooked

Heat oil in large skillet on medium-high heat. Add sausage; cook and stir until lightly browned. Add chicken, onion, pepper, celery and garlic; cook and stir until chicken is cooked through.

Add tomatoes, okra, tomato sauce and seasoning; bring to boil, stirring occasionally to break apart okra. Stir in rice; cover. Remove from heat. Let stand 5 minutes. Stir.

Makes 6 servings.

MY MOTHER NEZZIE BECKETT HEATH SAID...

"Be polite to other people." She lived this as an example for me.

Jacquelyn Heath Parker
Crete, IL

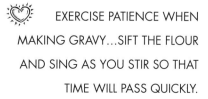 EXERCISE PATIENCE WHEN MAKING GRAVY...SIFT THE FLOUR AND SING AS YOU STIR SO THAT TIME WILL PASS QUICKLY.

CHICKEN & DUMPLINGS

There were seven of us, five children and my parents. We grew up outside of Cincinnati in Lincoln Heights. My Mother's chicken and dumplings was served mostly on Sundays when we were growing up. It was a frequently featured main dish and was usually accompanied by greens or string beans. On Sundays, we went to church and when we came back, we sat down to dinner as a family. My father said grace and then we ate. I remember that the chicken and dumplings were always welcome and delicious.

Dorothy Grier
Cincinnati, Ohio

ELOISE'S CHICKEN & DUMPLINGS

- **8 cups water**
- **1 broiler-fryer chicken (about 3 pounds)**
- **1 teaspoon celery flakes**
- **1 teaspoon pepper**
- **1 teaspoon poultry seasoning**
- **¾ teaspoon salt, divided**
- **2 cups flour**
- **¼ teaspoon baking powder**
- **1 package (10 ounces) frozen peas and carrots, thawed**

Bring water, chicken, celery flakes, pepper, poultry seasoning and ½ teaspoon of the salt to boil in large saucepot. Simmer, covered, 1 hour or until chicken is tender. Drain, reserving liquid. Cool chicken slightly. Remove chicken from bones and skin; chop chicken. Discard bones and skin.

Mix 2 cups of the flour, baking powder and remaining ¼ teaspoon salt. Add ¼ cup reserved liquid to flour mixture; stir until soft dough forms, adding additional liquid, if necessary.

Knead dough gently on lightly floured surface until smooth. Roll until dough is ¼ inch thick. Cut into 1x3-inch strips.

Bring remaining liquid to boil in saucepot. Add dumplings; simmer, uncovered, 20 minutes. Add chopped chicken and peas and carrots; cook until heated through.

Makes 6 servings.

CHICKEN & DUMPLINGS

1 **broiler-fryer chicken, cut into pieces (3 pounds)**
2 **stalks celery, cut into 1-inch pieces**
3 **carrots, cut into 1-inch pieces**
1 **medium onion, quartered**
1½ **teaspoons salt**
¼ **teaspoon pepper**
½ **cup flour**
2 **tablespoons cold water**
1 **egg white**

Bring chicken, water to cover, vegetables, salt and pepper to boil in large saucepot. Reduce heat; simmer 30 minutes or until chicken is tender. Remove chicken and vegetables; set aside. Discard celery and onion.

Mix flour, water and egg white in small bowl until stiff dough forms. Roll on lightly floured surface until dough is ⅛ inch thick. Cut into 1-inch strips.

Bring remaining liquid to boil in saucepot. Add dumplings; return chicken and carrots to pot. Cook on medium-high heat 10 to 15 minutes or until dumplings are tender.

Makes 6 servings.
Rosa L. Parks,
Civil Rights Activist

♡ WHEN MAKING CHICKEN & DUMPLINGS, ALWAYS DROP THE DOUGH STRIPS INTO THE POT WHILE THE CHICKEN AND BROTH ARE BOILING...DO NOT STIR THE DUMPLINGS UNTIL THEY ARE ALMOST TENDER.

MY MOTHER ANNA PEARL "WILLIE" BROOKS SAID...

"You can't buy love, you can't buy friendship, the most important things in life are free. Love is the most important; understanding, the greatest; trust is highly essential and kindness rules the world."

Catherine "Kitty" McElroy Brooks
Newark, NJ

CHICKEN CASSEROLE

2 cups elbow macaroni, uncooked
2 cups diced cooked chicken
2 stalks celery, chopped
1 cup mayonnaise
1 can (10¾ ounces) condensed cream of chicken soup, undiluted
1 small onion, chopped
¼ cup chicken broth
2 tablespoons chopped pimiento
¼ teaspoon pepper
¼ cup (1 ounce) Kraft natural shredded cheddar cheese

Preheat oven to 350°F. Grease 3-quart casserole.

Prepare macaroni as directed on package; drain. Mix macaroni, chicken, celery, mayonnaise, soup, onion, broth, pimiento and pepper. Pour into prepared casserole.

Bake 25 minutes. Top with cheese. Bake 5 minutes or until cheese is melted.

Makes 10 servings.

HERB & LEMON CHICKEN

6 chicken breast halves
1 teaspoon Worcestershire sauce
½ teaspoon garlic powder
½ teaspoon salt
¼ teaspoon pepper
1 tablespoon Dijon mustard
1 cup chicken broth
1 tablespoon lemon juice
3 bay leaves
2 tablespoons flour

Heat oven to 350°F.

Place chicken in Dutch oven or roasting pan with cover. Sprinkle with Worcestershire, garlic powder, salt, and pepper. Brush chicken with mustard. Add broth, lemon juice and bay leaves to pot; cover.

Bake 1 hour or until chicken is cooked through. To thicken pan juices, remove chicken from pot. Whisk in flour; bring to boil on high heat. Reduce heat to low; simmer until thickened. Serve over chicken.

Makes 6 servings.

CHICKEN & WILD RICE CASSEROLE

1 **package (6¾ ounces) Minute long grain and wild rice**
3 **cups chopped cooked chicken**
1 **can (16 ounces) French-style green beans, drained**
1 **can (10¾ ounces) condensed cream of celery soup, undiluted**
½ **cup Kraft real mayonnaise**
1 **can (4 ounces) water chestnuts, drained, sliced**
2 **tablespoons chopped pimiento**
2 **tablespoons finely chopped onion**

Prepare rice as directed on package.

Heat oven to 350°F.

Mix rice and remaining ingredients in 13x9-inch baking pan.

Bake 40 minutes or until heated through.

Makes 8 servings.

MY MOTHERS LILLIAN AND BEA SAID...

I was blessed to have two mothers. They both had strong influences on me. They also had strong sense of self, family, God and community, sharing, helping and nurturing, and firmness with love.

They made me understand that people must love themselves before they can pass that love on to others; that life is a precious gift to be enjoyed, to be realistic, not negative and know that what you put out there you get back.

Nancy Wilson
Song Stylist

BAKED CHICKEN & RICE CASSEROLE

1½ teaspoons cider vinegar
1 teaspoon salt
½ teaspoon pepper
½ teaspoon paprika
1 package (1¼ ounces) onion soup mix, divided
8 chicken pieces
¼ cup (½ stick) Parkay spread stick or butter
1 can (10¾ ounces) condensed cream of mushroom soup, undiluted
2¼ cups Minute original or premium rice, uncooked

Mix vinegar, salt, pepper, paprika and 1 teaspoon of the onion soup mix in small bowl. Sprinkle over chicken. Melt spread in large skillet on medium heat. Add chicken; brown on both sides. Set aside.

Place condensed cream of mushroom soup in 4-cup measuring cup; add water to make 3 cups. Stir in remaining onion soup mix. Place rice, chicken and 1½ cups of the soup mixture in 3-quart baking dish. Top with chicken. Pour remaining 1½ cups soup mix mixture over chicken; cover.

Bake 1 hour or until chicken is cooked through.

Makes 4 servings.

MY MOTHER VALARIE TRIGG LAW SAID...

"Faith and works are like the light and heat of a candle; they can't be separated."

**Louise Trigg Barnes
Charleston, SC**

♥ SEASON CUT-UP CHICKEN FOR FRYING AND PLACE IN THE REFRIGERATOR FOR 1-2 HOURS BEFORE DREDGING IN THE FLOUR...THIS ALLOWS THE CHICKEN TO ABSORB THE SEASONINGS.

FRIED CHICKEN

If it's Sunday, and it's dinner, one thing that is virtually guaranteed to be on the table is fried chicken. There may be ham and there may be pork chops, but there WILL be fried chicken.

There are many ways to fry chicken. Some cooks bread the chicken with a milk-bound batter, while others simply roll the pieces in a mixture of cornmeal and seasonings. The results, though differing in taste according to method and seasoning, are invariably delicious. For many of us, fried chicken wouldn't be fried chicken without rice and gravy to go with it, but there are those who like it dry as well.

Any good African-American cook will tell you that, in order to fry truly great chicken, you need a heavy, black, cast-iron skillet. They're right. People go on about how the cast iron conducts the heat evenly so that it cooks better, and that's true. But, for some of us, the cast-iron skillet is more than a cooking tool. It's a link to the past and to the history of the hands that have fried chicken in iron skillets for generations.

—Jessica B. Harris

SOUTHERN FRIED CHICKEN

3½ **pounds chicken pieces**	Sprinkle chicken with salt and pepper. Refrigerate 30 minutes. Place flour in paper or plastic bag. Add chicken pieces, 1 or 2 at a time; shake to coat.
1½ **teaspoons salt**	
¼ **teaspoon pepper**	
1 **cup flour**	
1½ **cups shortening**	

Melt shortening in large cast-iron skillet on high heat. Add chicken, skin side down a few pieces at a time; cook 15 minutes on each side or until cooked through and golden brown. Drain on paper towels; keep warm. Repeat with remaining chicken.

Makes 8 servings.

HERITAGE RECIPE

QUICK CHICKEN STIR-FRY

½ cup **Miracle Whip salad dressing,** divided
4 **boneless skinless chicken breast halves (about 1¼ pounds), cut into strips**
¼ **teaspoon garlic powder**
1 **package (16 ounces) frozen mixed vegetables, thawed**
3 **tablespoons soy sauce**
Hot cooked rice

Heat 2 tablespoons of the dressing in large skillet on medium-high heat. Add chicken and garlic powder; stir-fry 3 minutes or until lightly browned.

Stir in vegetables; cook and stir 3 to 5 minutes or until chicken is cooked through and vegetables are thoroughly heated.

Reduce heat to medium. Stir in remaining dressing and soy sauce; simmer 1 minute. Serve over rice.

Makes 4 servings.

CREOLE-STYLE CHICKEN BAKE

1 **can (16 ounces) black eye peas, drained**
1 **can (14½ ounces) stewed tomatoes**
1 **package (10 ounces) frozen cut okra, thawed**
2½ **pounds chicken pieces**
1 **envelope Shake 'N Bake seasoning and coating mixture — hot 'n spicy recipe for chicken**

Heat oven to 400°F.

Mix peas, tomatoes and okra in 13x9-inch baking dish. Coat chicken with coating mixture as directed on package. Arrange in single layer over tomato mixture.

Bake 50 minutes or until cooked through.

Makes 6 servings.

MY MOTHER JACQUELYN "JACKIE" PARKER SAID...

"Good manners are a sign of good home training."

Kimberly Dawn Parker
Crete, IL

HONEY MUSTARD CHICKEN

½ cup **Miracle Whip salad dressing**
2 tablespoons **Dijon mustard**
1 tablespoon **honey**
4 **boneless skinless chicken breast halves**

Heat broiler.

Mix salad dressing, mustard and honey in small bowl. Place chicken on rack of broiler pan. Brush with ½ of the dressing mixture. Broil 5 inches from heat 16 to 20 minutes or until chicken is cooked through, turning once and brushing with remaining salad dressing mixture.

Makes 4 servings.

Note: Chicken can be grilled. Heat grill. Place chicken on greased grill over hot coals. Grill 16 to 20 minutes or until chicken is cooked through, turning once and brushing with remaining salad dressing mixture.

CHICKEN BARBADOS

1 teaspoon **grated orange peel (optional)**
1 envelope **Shake 'N Bake seasoning and coating mixture — original recipe for chicken**
2½ pounds **chicken pieces**
2 **bananas**
⅓ cup **orange juice**
½ cup **firmly packed brown sugar**
Toasted Baker's Angel Flake coconut

Heat oven to 450°F.

Mix orange peel and coating mixture; coat chicken with coating mixture as directed on package. Arrange in single layer in shallow baking pan.

Bake 40 to 45 minutes or until cooked through. Meanwhile, peel bananas and cut in half lengthwise; dip in orange juice and roll in brown sugar. Reduce oven temperature to 350°F. Place bananas around chicken; bake 10 minutes. Garnish with coconut.

Makes 6 servings.

CHICKEN WITH CURRIED VEGETABLES

3 tablespoons oil
1 pound chicken pieces
1 large onion, chopped
1 teaspoon minced jalapeño pepper
1 teaspoon curry powder
2 large tomatoes, finely chopped
1 chicken bouillon cube
¾ teaspoon salt
½ teaspoon pepper
1 package (10 ounces) frozen mixed vegetables
Hot cooked rice

Heat oil in large saucepot on medium-high heat. Add chicken; brown on both sides. Remove chicken. Add onion and jalapeño pepper; cook and stir until tender. Stir in curry powder; cook 1 minute.

Return chicken to pot. Add tomatoes, bouillon cube, salt, pepper and vegetables; bring to boil. Reduce heat to low; cover and simmer 20 minutes or until chicken is tender. Serve over rice.

Makes 4 servings.

MY MOTHER VELMA LEE MOORE SAID...

"Always look your best," my Mother told me. "First impressions are lasting. In a society where Blacks are not held in high esteem, you can't afford to be dismissed simply because of your clothes and appearance."

Congresswoman Maxine Waters
State of California

POT LUCK CHICKEN CASSEROLE

4 tablespoons (½ stick) Parkay spread stick or butter, divided
⅓ cup chopped pecans
1 package (6 ounces) Stove Top cornbread stuffing mix
1⅔ cups water
2 cups diced cooked smoked chicken or turkey
½ cup diced ham
1 bunch green onions
1 hard-cooked egg, chopped

Heat oven to 350°F. Place 2 tablespoons of the margarine in 2-quart casserole.

Bake 5 minutes or until spread is melted. Stir in pecans. Bake 10 minutes or until lightly browned. Set aside.

Mix contents of vegetable/seasoning packet, water and remaining 2 tablespoons margarine in medium saucepan. Bring to boil. Reduce heat to low; cover and simmer 5 minutes. Stir in stuffing crumbs; cover. Remove from heat. Let stand 5 minutes. Stir in remaining ingredients. Spoon into casserole.

Bake 20 minutes or until heated through.

Makes 4 servings.

☼♡ FREEZE LEFTOVER CHICKEN OR BEEF STOCK IN ICE TRAYS. THEN REMOVE THE FROZEN CUBES, PLACE IN PLASTIC BAGS AND STORE IN FREEZER FOR FUTURE USE.

OUR MOTHER LEONA BROWN DANIEL SAID...

"Don't let the lack of knowledge and lack of skill keep you down. If you don't take advantage of an education, you have no one to blame but yourself."
Dr. Ida Daniel Dark and Dr. John T. Daniel, Jr.
Philadelphia, PA

CHICKEN NOODLE BAKE

3½ to 4 pounds chicken pieces
4 cups water
1 tablespoon salt
2 onions, sliced
1 carrot, sliced
6 celery leaves
6 whole peppercorns
1 clove garlic, minced
2 tablespoons oil
1 cup chopped celery
1 cup chopped green pepper
⅓ cup flour
3 pimientos, chopped
½ teaspoon ground red pepper
1 package (16 ounces) medium noodles, cooked, drained
2 cups shredded cheddar cheese
Paprika

Bring chicken, water, salt, onions, carrot, celery leaves, peppercorns and garlic to boil in large saucepot. Reduce heat to low; simmer 1 hour or until chicken is tender. Remove chicken; cool slightly. Remove chicken from bones and skin. Cut into 1-inch pieces; reserve. Strain broth; discard vegetables and seasonings. Cool broth; skim off fat.

Heat oil in large skillet. Add chopped celery and green pepper; cook and stir until tender. Stir in flour. Gradually stir in reserved broth until smooth. Stirring constantly, cook on medium heat until mixture boils and thickens. Stir in pimientos, red pepper and reserved chicken.

Heat oven to 375°F. Grease 4-quart casserole dish. Place noodles in prepared dish. Pour chicken mixture over noodles. Toss lightly until well mixed. Sprinkle with cheese and paprika.

Bake 40 minutes or until bubbly. Sprinkle with additional paprika.

Makes 12 servings.
Dr. Jeanne L. Noble,
Professor,
The City University of New York

MY MOTHER MYRTLE HARVEY SCOTT SAID...
"Always decorate your table and your food to please the eyes."
Leonidis H. Walker
Harbor City, CA

OPEN-FACED GRILLED CHICKEN SANDWICHES

1 **cup mayonnaise**
1 **tablespoon honey**
1 **tablespoon lemon juice**
¼ **teaspoon dried thyme leaves**
Foccacia
1 **boneless skinless chicken breast half, grilled**
Salt and pepper
Fried leeks
Risotto cakes

Mix mayonnaise, honey, lemon juice and thyme in medium bowl.

Trim a slice of the foccacia so that it is the same size as grilled chicken breast. Toast or grill foccacia.

Spread mayonnaise mixture over foccacia. Top with chicken. Season to taste with salt and pepper. Garnish with fried leeks and serve with risotto cakes. Refrigerate leftover mayonnaise mixture for another use.

Makes 1 serving.
Carol Moseley-Braun,
Senator,
State of Illinois

PARMESAN CHICKEN

1 **cup Miracle Whip salad dressing**
½ **cup (2 ounces) Kraft 100% grated Parmesan cheese**
2 **teaspoons dried oregano leaves**
1 **broiler-fryer chicken, cut up (3 to 3½ pounds)**

Heat oven to 375°F.

Mix salad dressing, cheese and oregano.

Place chicken in 13x9-inch baking dish. Spread with salad dressing mixture.

Bake 40 to 45 minutes or until cooked through.

Makes 4 servings.

MY MOTHER LUELLEN TURNER...
Always prayed before she prepared her food.

Mattie L. Haywood
Jacksonville, FL

POT ROAST WITH PRUNES

3	tablespoons oil
1	boneless beef chuck or rump roast (4 pounds)
2	medium onions, sliced
1	large clove garlic, minced
1½	cups pitted prunes
1⅓	cups water, divided
1	cup dry red wine
2	teaspoons salt
¼	teaspoon pepper
4	whole cloves
2	tablespoons flour

Heat oil in 8-quart saucepot or Dutch oven on medium-high heat. Add meat; brown on all sides. Remove meat from pot. Add onions and garlic; cook and stir until tender. Return meat to pot. Add prunes, 1 cup of the water, wine, salt, pepper and cloves; bring to boil. Reduce heat to low; cover and simmer 3 to 3½ hours or until meat is tender.

Place meat and prunes on serving platter. Stir flour and remaining ⅓ cup water in small bowl. Gradually stir into liquid in saucepot. Cook on medium heat, stirring frequently, until thickened. Serve with meat.

Makes 12 servings.

CREAMY BEEF & MACARONI

1	pound ground beef
1	jar (30 ounces) spaghetti sauce
1	package (7 ounces) elbow macaroni, cooked, drained
½	cup Miracle Whip salad dressing
1	cup (4 ounces) Kraft natural shredded cheddar cheese

Brown meat; drain.

Stir in spaghetti sauce, macaroni and dressing; cook on medium heat 15 minutes or until heated through.

Sprinkle with cheese.

Makes 4 servings.

MY MOTHER ELIZA "MAMA LIZA" NESBITT SAID...

"Be careful of what you pray for because you may get it."

**Armentha Nesbitt
Cleveland, OH**

MAGGIE BURGERS WITH CABBAGE RELISH

1½ **pounds ground beef**
½ **teaspoon garlic powder**
¼ **teaspoon pepper**

Cabbage Relish:
2 **cups shredded cabbage**
1½ **large dill pickles, chopped (about ¾ cup)**
¼ **cup sweet pickle relish**
¼ **cup prepared mustard**
½ **teaspoon sugar**

Heat broiler.

Shape meat into 6 patties. Sprinkle with garlic powder and pepper. Place patties on rack of broiler pan. Broil 3 to 5 inches from heat 4 minutes on each side or to desired doneness.

Meanwhile, mix cabbage, pickles, relish, mustard and sugar in medium bowl. Serve burgers topped with relish.

Makes 6 servings.

SPANISH LIVER

¼ **cup flour**
¼ **teaspoon salt**
⅛ **teaspoon pepper**
¼ **cup (½ stick) margarine or butter**
1 **pound sliced beef liver**
1 **medium onion, chopped**
1 **medium green pepper, chopped**
1 **can (14½ ounces) stewed tomatoes**
1 **can (8 ounces) tomato sauce**
  Hot cooked rice

Mix flour, salt and pepper; coat meat. Shake off excess.

Melt margarine in large skillet on medium-high heat. Add meat; brown on both sides. Remove from skillet. Cut into 1½-inch chunks.

Add pepper and onion to skillet; cook and stir until tender. Add tomatoes, sauce and meat; cook 7 minutes or until meat is cooked through. Serve over hot rice.

Makes 4 servings.

MEATLOAF

This recipe is so simple and so tasty that it has become one of those things that people expect. When we were having family over, my Mother would just double the ingredients because everybody loved it so much. Meatloaf also got taken to potluck suppers and family dinners. Today, everyone in the family knows about the meatloaf, so it is usually something that gets asked for.

Jeannine Ward
Inglewood, California

SCRUMPTIOUS MEATLOAF

1	**egg**
½	**cup catsup**
1	**pound ground beef**
½	**pound ground pork**
1	**cup fresh bread crumbs**
1	**medium onion, finely chopped**
1	**small green pepper, finely chopped**
1½	**teaspoons salt**
½	**teaspoon pepper**
1	**can (8 ounces) tomato sauce**
1½	**tablespoons firmly packed brown sugar**
1½	**tablespoons cider vinegar**
1	**tablespoon prepared mustard**
1	**teaspoon Worcestershire sauce**

Heat oven to 350°F.

Beat egg and catsup in large bowl. Add beef, pork, crumbs, onion, green pepper, salt and pepper; mix well. Shape into oval loaf in 12x8-inch baking dish.

Stir tomato sauce, sugar, vinegar, mustard and Worcestershire in small bowl. Brush ½ of the sauce over meatloaf.

Bake 1 hour 15 minutes or until cooked through, brushing occasionally with remaining sauce. Discard any remaining sauce.

Makes 6 servings.

MY MOTHER MAELENA HARDMAN SAID...

"Education is the key to success."

Corlista H. Hardman

BARBECUE MEATBALLS & VEGETABLES

½ cup Kraft original barbecue sauce
½ cup Miracle Whip salad dressing
¼ cup honey
3 teaspoons chili powder, divided
1 teaspoon each ground red pepper, black pepper and salt
1 pound ground beef
1 green pepper, cut into chunks
1 onion, sliced
1 cup sliced mushrooms
1 cup sliced yellow squash
1 cup sliced zucchini
1 can (8 ounces) pineapple chunks, drained
2 tablespoons chopped fresh parsley
Hot cooked pasta

Mix barbecue sauce, salad dressing, honey, 2 teaspoons of the chili powder and ½ teaspoon *each* of the ground red pepper, pepper and salt. Set aside.

Mix meat, remaining 1 teaspoon chili powder and remaining ½ teaspoon *each* ground red pepper, pepper and salt. Shape into 12 meatballs.

Brown meatballs in large skillet on medium-high heat; drain on paper towels. Add green pepper, onion, mushrooms, squash, zucchini and pineapple to skillet; cook and stir on medium heat 5 minutes or until tender. Stir in reserved barbecue sauce mixture and meatballs. Reduce heat to low; cover and simmer 15 minutes or until heated through. Stir in parsley. Serve over hot cooked pasta.

Makes 6 servings.

MY MOTHER MARY LAURENZA SUSAN JOHNSON WHITE SAID...

"Always trust God because he would never leave me or forsake me and to search for the good in all those I meet."

Marilyn E. White
Inglewood, CA

ENCHILADA PIE CASSEROLE

2	tablespoons oil
1	pound ground beef
1	medium onion, chopped
1	green pepper, chopped
1	can (6 ounces) tomato sauce
½	cup water
2	teaspoons garlic salt
2	tablespoons chili powder
2	teaspoons ground cumin
1	teaspoon ground red pepper
1	can (4 ounces) pitted ripe olives, drained, chopped
4	green onions, chopped
8	corn tortillas
1½	cups shredded cheddar cheese

Heat oven to 400°F.

Heat oil in large skillet on medium heat. Add meat, onion and green pepper; cook and stir until meat is browned and vegetables are tender. Add tomato sauce, water and seasonings; simmer 3 to 5 minutes or until slightly thickened. Reserve ½ cup of the meat sauce.

Layer tortillas, remaining meat sauce, olives and onions in 1½-quart casserole. Repeat layers. Top with cheese; cover.

Bake 20 to 25 minutes or until cheese is melted. Cool. Cut into wedges. Top with reserved meat sauce.

Makes 6 servings.
Margaret Warren,
Imperial Commandress,
Imperial Court Daughter of Iris
1991-1993

♥ ADDING KETCHUP AND MUSTARD TO GROUND BEEF PUTS FLAVOR INTO HAMBURGERS.

MY MOTHER MARGARET JOHNSON "MUTDEAR" FRANCOIS SAID...

"You can win a man by cooking delicious dishes and never go to bed angry with your husband." She was right....I have been married 34 years.

Claudette Francois Sweet
Denver, CO

GRITS

There were eight of us; I was the oldest girl. I always observed my Mother cooking. Sometimes, when things were low, she'd put together a bit of this and a bit of that and make a big meal for us. She'd stretch things, and yet it would be a meal where everyone got an even portion. She would always see to it that everyone got an equal amount. This was really important, as there were eight children. She'd use just a little to make a lot. It helped us through the difficult times when we had to save a dollar.

Claudette Francois Sweet
Denver, Colorado

MUTDEAR GRITS CASSEROLE

1½ **pounds bulk pork sausage, crumbled**
½ **pound Oscar Mayer bacon**
2 **cups quick-cooking grits**
1 **medium green pepper, chopped**
½ **bunch green onions, sliced**
1 **medium onion, chopped**
1 **clove garlic, minced**
6 **eggs, beaten**
2 **cups (8 ounces) shredded Kraft natural cheddar cheese, divided**

Heat oven to 375°F.

Brown sausage in large skillet on medium-high heat. Drain. Remove sausage; drain on paper towels. Cook bacon in skillet on medium-high heat until crisp, turning frequently. Drain, reserving 2 tablespoons drippings in skillet.

Prepare grits as directed on package. Spread ½ in 3-quart shallow casserole. Top with sausage and bacon.

Heat reserved drippings in skillet on medium-high heat. Add green pepper, green onions, onion and garlic; cook and stir until tender. Add eggs; cook until eggs are set, stirring occasionally. Break apart eggs; add to casserole. Top with 1½ cups of the cheese and remaining grits.

Bake 40 minutes or until heated through. Top with remaining ½ cup cheese.

Makes 8 servings.

BLESS MY SOUL CHOPS

6 tablespoons margarine or butter, divided
1 medium onion, chopped
1 stalk celery, chopped
1 clove garlic, minced
2 cups crumbled cornbread
1 cup fresh bread crumbs
⅓ cup chopped fresh parsley
1 tablespoon poultry seasoning
¼ teaspoon salt
Dash pepper
1 egg, beaten
6 pork chops with pockets, about 1½ inches thick
1 cup apple juice
½ teaspoon dried basil leaves

Melt 4 tablespoons of the margarine in large skillet on medium-high heat. Add onion, celery and garlic; cook and stir until tender. Mix cornbread, bread crumbs, parsley, poultry seasoning, salt and pepper in large bowl. Stir in egg and vegetable mixture. Stuff chops, securing with toothpicks, if necessary. Sprinkle with additional salt and pepper.

Melt remaining 2 tablespoons margarine in large skillet with cover or Dutch oven on medium-high heat. Add 3 of the chops; cook 5 minutes on each side or until browned. Repeat with remaining chops. Return chops to skillet. Add apple juice and basil; bring to boil. Reduce heat to low; cover and simmer 40 minutes or until chops are cooked through, turning once.

Makes 6 servings.

 SAUSAGE PATTIES ROLLED IN FLOUR WON'T CRACK OPEN DURING FRYING.

MY MOTHER GENEVA "TINY" HALL SAID...

"Under my roof, you are riding on the flowery beds of ease. Prepare yourself to meet the real world, for it surely awaits you. But the best help you will ever find will be at the end of your arm."

Velma Bagley
Mount Vernon, NY

SAUSAGE PEPPER POT

1 **pound hot or mild bulk sausage, crumbled**
1 **cup chopped green pepper**
1 **cup chopped red pepper**
1 **can (10½ ounces) condensed chicken broth, undiluted**
1 **cup water**
1 **cup frozen lima beans, thawed**
2 **cups Minute original or premium rice, uncooked**
1 **teaspoon paprika**

Cook and stir sausage and peppers in large skillet on medium heat until sausage is browned. Stir in broth, water and beans. Bring to boil. Stir in rice and paprika; cover. Remove from heat. Let stand 5 minutes. Stir.

Makes 4 servings.

HERITAGE RECIPE

MY MOTHER EDNA DAVIES MOSELEY SAID...

I remember "canning" summer fruit with my Mother. In our basement, she and her friends peeled and cored bushels of apples and pears and peaches. I remember the huge old stove with enormous pots bubbling like so many cauldrons. I felt fortunate to be a "helper," let in on an annual feminine ritual that was reserved for serious cooks. They sealed and boiled the fruit, the syrup, the Ball jars—the steam from the stove emitted a glorious, fragrant essence into our entire home—if not the block. When the long process was completed and all of the cleanup done, we were left with a couple dozen gleaming jars full of the treasure of a day's work well done. We were to enjoy the preserves for the rest of the year. Each time a new jar was opened, I would remember the day it was made.

Senator Carol Moseley-Braun
State of Illinois

PORK CUTLETS WITH SWEET POTATO DRESSING

1   medium sweet potato, peeled, cubed
7   tablespoons Parkay spread stick or butter, divided
¾   cup diced apple
½   cup sliced green onions
¼   cup firmly packed brown sugar
1   package (6 ounces) Stove Top stuffing mix for pork
1½ cups water
¼   teaspoon pepper
1   pound pork cutlets

Heat oven to 375°F.

Cook potato in boiling water 5 to 8 minutes or until tender. Drain; set aside.

Melt 1 tablespoon of the spread in large skillet on medium-high heat. Add apple, onions and sugar; cook and stir 2 minutes. Add potato; cook and stir 1 minute. Add 4 tablespoons of the spread, vegetable/seasoning packet and water; bring to boil. Remove from heat. Stir in stuffing crumbs and pepper; set aside.

Heat remaining 2 tablespoons spread in skillet on medium-high heat. Add pork; cook 3 to 4 minutes on each side or until browned. Place in 9-inch square baking pan. Spoon dressing mixture over pork.

Bake 20 minutes or until heated through.

Makes 6 servings.

MY MOTHER MAE "LITTLE MARY" SHORT SAID...

"My job is to provide for your shelter, clothing and food. Your job is to go to school, get an education and then provide the same support for your children."

Debbie Short Craddock
Bowie, MD

SMOTHERED PORK CHOPS

6 **pork chops, ½ inch thick**
1 **envelope Shake 'N Bake seasoning and coating mixture — original recipe for pork**
2 **large onions, thickly sliced**
1 **tablespoon oil**
2 **cans (10 ounces each) pork gravy**

Heat oven to 425°F.

Coat chops with coating mixture as directed on package. Place in 13x9-inch baking pan. Mix onions and oil in medium bowl; place over chops.

Bake 30 minutes. Reduce oven temperature to 350°F. Pour gravy over chops; cover. Bake 30 minutes or until cooked through.

Makes 6 servings.

BAKED PORK CHOPS

6 **lean center-cut pork chops, ½ inch thick**
1 **egg white**
1 **cup evaporated milk**
1 **cup corn flake crumbs**
¼ **cup dry bread crumbs**
2 **tablespoons Creole or Cajun seasoning**
½ **teaspoon salt No stick cooking spray**

Heat oven to 375°F. Spray 13x9-inch baking pan with cooking spray.

Place chops in shallow baking dish. Beat egg white and milk in small bowl; pour over chops. Let stand 5 minutes, turning once.

Mix crumbs and seasonings in pie plate or shallow pan; coat chops. Place chops in prepared pan.

Bake 40 minutes or until cooked through, turning halfway through baking time.

Makes 6 servings.
**Johnny Rivers,
Executive Chef,
Walt DisneyWorld Resorts**

MY MOTHER, EVELYN H. SIMMONS SAID...

"I keep having this dream of standing in a big hall watching you graduate from college."

**Barbara VanBlake
Washington, DC**

BILLY'S RIBS

Ribs:
- 10 **pounds pork baby back ribs**
- 2 **quarts water**
- 2 **medium onions, chopped**
- ¼ **cup liquid hickory smoke**
- 2 **tablespoons salt**
- 1 **tablespoon pepper**
- 1 **teaspoon onion salt**
- 1 **clove garlic, sliced**
  Dash paprika

Sauce:
- 8 **cups assorted purchased barbecue sauces**
- 1 **bottle (14 ounces) catsup**
- 1 **bottle (12 ounces) beer**
- 1 **onion, chopped**
- 2 **hot chili peppers**
- 1 **tablespoon firmly packed brown sugar**
- 1 **clove garlic, sliced**
- 1 **teaspoon seasoning salt**

For ribs, mix ribs, water, onions, liquid smoke, salt, pepper, onion salt, garlic and paprika in large saucepot; cover. Refrigerate overnight to marinate.

For sauce, mix barbecue sauces, ketchup, beer, onion, peppers, brown sugar, garlic and seasoning salt in large saucepan. Simmer on low heat 1 hour.

Heat grill.

Drain ribs. Discard any remaining marinade. Brush ribs thoroughly with sauce.

Place ribs on grill over hot coals. Grill 1 to 1½ hours or until cooked through, turning and basting frequently with sauce.

Makes 8 servings.
**Marilyn McCoo-Davis,
Entertainer**

MY MOTHER EUNICE MIDDLETON LEFTENANT SAID...

"Be your own person. Do the very best you can all the time and let God do the rest."

**Mary E. Leftenant
Amityville, NY**

RED HOT RICE & PORK

1 can (14½ ounces) stewed tomatoes, undrained
1 can (8 ounces) tomato sauce
3 slices Oscar Mayer bacon, cut into small pieces
1 pound boneless pork, cut into ½-inch cubes
1 medium onion, chopped
1 small red pepper, chopped
1 tablespoon hot pepper sauce
⅓ cup stuffed green olives, thinly sliced
½ teaspoon garlic powder
2 cups Minute original or premium rice, uncooked

Drain stewed tomatoes, reserving liquid. Mix reserved liquid and tomato sauce in measuring cup. Add water to make 2 cups; set aside.

Cook bacon in large skillet on medium-high heat until partially cooked. Add pork; cook and stir until pork and bacon are cooked through. Add onion and red pepper; cook and stir until tender.

Stir in tomatoes, measured liquids, hot pepper sauce, olives and garlic powder; bring to boil. Stir in rice; cover. Remove from heat. Let stand 5 minutes. Stir.

Makes 4 servings.

MY MOTHER EULA MAE "SHANG" MITCHELL SAID...

"It made no difference what others said about me or how they felt about me. I was her child and she would always love me."

Maggie Jean Gardner
Passaic, NJ

 BRUSH FRESH MEAT WITH OLIVE OIL BEFORE WRAPPING FOR FREEZER. IT WILL KEEP THE MEAT MOIST.

CHITLINS

To some, they're an acquired taste. To others, they're a dish fit for a queen. To all of us, whether we eat them or not, they're a taste of our history. Chitterlings, or chitlins as we really call them, are the pig's innards. Like so many elements of African-American cooking, these unwanted parts were taken, scrupulously cleaned, seasoned, cooked, and transformed into a delicacy with loving attention.

Anyone who has ever cooked chitlins knows that their preparation is time-consuming and arduous, for each little fold and wrinkle must be thoroughly washed and then scrubbed and scrubbed again before they're fit for a gourmet. But if you love them, then it's worth it.

Whether they're boiled in a potently pungent pot or lightly breaded in cornmeal and flour and then deep fried, chitlins are a part of our past. For many, they're a part of our present as well, especially during the holiday season, when buckets of them are sold at supermarkets and butcher shops. It's only fitting after all, that during the holiday season, we remember the past and the chitlins and other dishes that helped our ancestors survive so that we could be here today to celebrate.

—**Jessica B. Harris**

CHITLINS

10 pounds frozen chitlins, thawed
¼ cup vinegar
1 large potato, cut in half
2 medium onions, quartered
1 stalk celery, cut into thirds
2 cloves garlic
1 tablespoon salt
2 bay leaves
½ teaspoon crushed red pepper
Hot cooked rice
Hot pepper sauce

To clean chitlins, wash and scrub, using small brush, in warm water in sink. Rub to remove excess fat and residue. Wash and rinse several times until water runs clear. Drain.

Bring chitlins, cold water to cover, vinegar, potato, onions, celery, garlic, salt, bay leaves, and red pepper to boil in large saucepot on high heat. Reduce heat to medium; cover and simmer 1½ to 2 hours or until tender. Remove potato; discard. Remove chitlins from saucepot; cool slightly. Cut into pieces. Serve over rice with hot pepper sauce.

Makes 12 servings.

HERITAGE RECIPE

COUNTRY SOUSE MEAT

6 pigs feet
1½ pounds pork snouts
1 large onion, quartered
2 stalks celery, cut into thirds
2 bay leaves
2½ teaspoons salt
¾ teaspoon pepper
2 teaspoons dried thyme leaves
⅓ cup vinegar
Crackers

Bring meat, salted water to cover, onion, celery and bay leaves to boil in large saucepot. Reduce heat to low; cover and simmer 2 hours or until meat falls from bones. Drain, reserving 1 cup liquid; discard vegetables and bay leaves. Cool meat slightly. Remove from bones. Cut into small pieces. Discard bones.

Mix meat, salt, pepper, thyme, reserved liquid and vinegar in large bowl. Pour into 9x5-inch loaf pan; cover with aluminum foil. Place heavy object such as 16 ounce can of vegetables on top.

Refrigerate overnight or until firm. Slice loaf thinly. Serve with additional vinegar and crackers.

Makes 12 servings.

HERITAGE RECIPE

♥ SLICE WHITE POTATOES AND COOK WITH CHITLINS TO CUT DOWN ON AROMA.

MY MOTHER LESLIE COBB SAID...

To all my sisters and me, "Don't call or chase after boys. Let them make the first move, and then you will know they really care." We are now all happily married.

Cathy Cobb Halford
Ridgeland, MS

FRIED BRAINS

¾ **pound calf brains**
½ **cup flour**
1 **egg**
1 **tablespoon water**
½ **cup cornmeal**
1 **teaspoon garlic salt**
½ **teaspoon pepper**
¼ **cup oil**

Soak brains in cold water to cover in medium bowl 2 hours. Remove any skins. Place brains in medium bowl; add boiling water to cover. Let stand 20 minutes. Drain.

Cut brains in two, lengthwise. Beat egg and 1 tablespoon water in small bowl. Mix cornmeal, garlic salt and pepper in plastic bag. Add brains; shake to coat.

Heat oil in large skillet. Add brains; cook on both sides until golden. Drain on paper towels.

Makes 4 servings.

TROTTERS IN TOMATO SAUCE

6 **pigs feet*, cleaned**
1 **cup vinegar**
1 **tablespoon salt**
2 **bay leaves**
1 **clove garlic**
2 **cans (15 ounces each) tomato sauce**
2 **medium onions, quartered**
2 **medium green peppers, sliced**
1 **teaspoon dried oregano leaves**

*Or use 6 split pigs feet.

Bring meat, cold water to cover, vinegar, salt, bay leaves and garlic to boil in large saucepot. Reduce heat to medium; simmer 1½ hours. Drain, reserving 2 cups liquid. Return reserved liquid and meat to pot. Add tomato sauce, onions, peppers and oregano. Cook 2 hours on medium heat or until meat is tender.

Makes 6 servings.

MY MOTHER LOUVENIA GILLS SAID...

"No matter what the situation, always speak softly and be a lady."

Josie M. Barrow
Oakland, CA

MACARONI & OYSTER CASSEROLE

3 tablespoons margarine or butter, divided
1½ cups chopped celery
3 medium onions, chopped
½ cup sliced mushrooms
2 tablespoons chopped fresh parsley
2½ cups elbow macaroni, cooked, drained
2 pints shucked oysters, liquor reserved
¾ cup milk
2 cups cracker meal

Heat oven to 375°F. Grease 3-quart baking dish.

Melt 2 tablespoons of the margarine in large skillet on medium-high heat. Add celery, onions and mushrooms; cook and stir until tender. Stir in parsley.

Layer ½ of the macaroni, oysters and liquor and onion mixture in prepared baking dish. Repeat layers. Pour milk over casserole. Top with cracker meal. Dot with remaining 1 tablespoon margarine.

Bake 35 to 40 minutes or until heated through.

Makes 8 servings.

CHARLESTON SHRIMP

1 pound medium shrimp, cleaned
2 tablespoons lemon juice
¼ teaspoon salt
⅛ teaspoon ground red pepper
2 tablespoons margarine or butter
¼ cup finely chopped onion
⅓ cup finely chopped green pepper
2 tablespoons flour
¾ cup chicken broth

Mix shrimp, lemon juice, salt and pepper in small bowl.

Melt margarine in large skillet on medium heat. Add onions, green pepper and shrimp mixture; cook and stir until shrimp are pink. Stir flour and broth in small bowl until smooth. Add to skillet; cook until sauce thickens, stirring occasionally.

Makes 2½ cups.

MOMMA'S DEVILED CRAB

2 tablespoons Parkay spread stick or butter
3 stalks celery, chopped
1 medium onion, chopped
1 medium green pepper, chopped
1 pound fresh crabmeat, cooked
½ cup Stove Top cornbread stuffing mix in the canister
1 teaspoon seafood seasoning
⅛ teaspoon Worcestershire sauce
Dash hot pepper sauce
3 eggs
½ cup Kraft real mayonnaise

Heat oven to 400°F.

Melt spread in large skillet on medium-high heat. Add celery, onion and green pepper; cook and stir until tender. Stir in crabmeat, stuffing mix, seafood seasoning, Worcestershire and pepper sauce; cover. Remove from heat.

Beat eggs in small bowl; stir in mayonnaise. Add to skillet; stir gently until well blended. Spoon mixture into individual crab shells or one 9-inch pie plate.

Bake 20 minutes or until heated through.

Makes 8 servings.

MY MOTHER PORTEA MARY COLLINS SAID...

"Hold your head high and back straight as no one can ride a straight back."

Marian F. Bell
Philadelphia, PA

SWEETIE'S SALMON CROQUETTES

2 cans (15½ ounces each) salmon, drained, flaked
¾ cup finely chopped onions
3 slices bread, crumbled
⅓ cup milk
2 eggs, slightly beaten
½ teaspoon salt
½ teaspoon pepper
3 tablespoons oil

Mix salmon, onions, bread, milk, eggs, salt and pepper in large bowl with fork. Shape into 16 patties.

Heat oil in large skillet over medium heat. Brown patties on both sides until golden.

Makes 8 servings.

MOZELLE'S GRILLED SALMON

1 envelope Good Seasons zesty Italian salad dressing mix
½ cup oil
¾ cup lemon juice
1½ tablespoons pepper
1 tablespoon Dijon mustard
1 teaspoon salt
1 clove garlic, minced
1 whole salmon (5 pounds), cleaned
¼ cup white wine

Bring salad dressing mix, oil, lemon juice, pepper, mustard, salt and garlic to boil in small saucepan on low heat; cover. Cool. Reserve ½ cup marinade; refrigerate. Pour remaining marinade over salmon in shallow dish; cover. Refrigerate at least 4 hours or overnight, turning occasionally, to marinate. Drain. Discard any remaining marinade.

Heat grill arranging charcoal with space in center for drip pan. (For gas grill, use low temperature.)

Stir ½ cup reserved marinade and wine in small bowl.

Grill salmon 1 hour or until tender, turning and brushing frequently with wine mixture.

Makes 10 servings.

DEVILED SALMON

3 tablespoons Parkay spread stick or butter
2 tablespoons finely chopped onion
2 tablespoons finely chopped green pepper
1 can (10¾ ounces) condensed tomato soup, undiluted
1 teaspoon lemon juice
1 teaspoon prepared mustard
½ teaspoon salt
1 can (15½ ounces) salmon, drained, flaked
1 cup Stove Top chicken flavor stuffing mix in the canister
3 tablespoons Parkay spread stick or butter, melted

Heat oven to 400°F.

Melt spread in medium saucepan on medium-high heat. Add onion and pepper; cook and stir until tender. Add soup, lemon juice, mustard and salt; simmer 3 minutes. Remove from heat. Gently stir in salmon. Mound mixture in 6 greased custard cups.

Toss stuffing mix and melted spread in small bowl; sprinkle over top.

Bake 10 to 15 minutes or until brown.

Makes 6 servings.

 FRESH FISH FREEZES IN A MILK CARTON FILLED WITH WATER.

MY MOTHER LUCY SHINER SAID...

"Lie, drink and steal....Lie in your own bed, drink cold water, and steal away from bad company. You will live a long life."

Mary E. Allen
Santa Monica, CA

FRIED FISH TART, TANGY, TASTY

6 red snapper fillets (about 1½ pounds)
2 tablespoons lemon juice
¼ teaspoon salt
 Dash pepper
6 tablespoons oil, divided
1 bunch green onions, sliced
½ cup cider vinegar
2 tablespoons hot pepper sauce
1 teaspoon pimento seed or whole allspice

Sprinkle fish with lemon juice, salt and pepper. Heat 2 tablespoons of the oil in large skillet on medium-high heat. Add fish 2 or 3 pieces at a time, skin side down; cook 5 minutes on each side or until fish is crisp and tender. Remove fish from skillet; keep warm. Repeat with remaining fish and 2 tablespoons of the oil, if necessary. Arrange fish in shallow baking dish.

Heat remaining 2 tablespoons oil in small saucepan on medium-high heat. Add onions; cook and stir until tender. Remove from heat. Mix in vinegar, pepper sauce and allspice. Pour over fish; cover. Refrigerate 2 hours. Serve cold.

Makes 6 servings.

SEAFOOD QUICHE

½ cup whipping cream
½ cup cottage cheese
4 eggs
½ teaspoon salt
¼ teaspoon pepper
¾ cup grated Swiss cheese
1 unbaked pastry shell (9 inch)
2 cups cooked crabmeat
 Dash ground nutmeg

Heat oven to 425°F.

Place cream, cottage cheese, eggs, salt and pepper in blender container; cover. Blend until smooth.

Sprinkle cheese in bottom of pastry shell. Top with crab. Pour cream mixture over crab; sprinkle with nutmeg.

Bake 15 minutes. Reduce oven temperature to 325°F. Bake 20 minutes or until set. Cover loosely with foil if quiche browns too quickly.

Makes 6 servings.

MIDDLE GEORGIA FRIED FISH

1½ **pounds mullet or other fish fillets**
1 **tablespoon pepper, divided**
1 **teaspoon salt, divided**
1 **cup yellow cornmeal**
2 **cups oil**

Rinse fish with water; pat dry. Sprinkle with 1 teaspoon of the pepper and ½ teaspoon of the salt.

Mix cornmeal and remaining 2 teaspoons pepper and ½ teaspoon salt; coat fish.

Heat oil in large skillet on medium-high heat. Add fish, 2 or 3 pieces at a time; cook 5 minutes on each side until golden brown and fish flakes easily with fork. Drain on paper towels; keep warm. Serve with hot sauce, mustard or catsup, if desired.

Makes 6 servings.

SHRIMP BALLS

1 **pound shrimp, cleaned, diced**
1 **egg, slightly beaten**
3 **green onions, finely chopped**
1½ **cups Stove Top chicken flavor stuffing mix in the canister, crushed**
2 **tablespoons chopped fresh parsley**
½ **cup flour**
⅓ **cup oil, divided**
1½ **cups water Hot cooked rice**

Mix shrimp, egg, onions, stuffing mix and parsley in large bowl. Shape into 12 (2-inch) balls. Coat with flour; shake off excess. Reserve flour.

Heat 4 tablespoons of the oil in large skillet over medium heat. Add shrimp balls; brown on all sides. Drain on paper towels.

Add remaining oil to skillet. Stir in reserved flour. Cook 2 minutes or until bubbling and brown. Gradually stir in water. Cook until flour mixture boils and thickens, stirring constantly. Reduce heat to low. Add shrimp balls; cook until heated through. Serve over rice.

Makes 4 servings.

CODFISH CAKES

1	**pound boneless salted cod**
2	**eggs**
3	**medium onions, finely chopped**
1	**large red pepper, chopped**
1	**large green pepper, chopped**
2	**cloves garlic, minced**
1	**tablespoon paprika**
2	**teaspoons ground black pepper**
	Dash ground red pepper
	Dash red pepper flakes
3	**cups flour**
1¾	**cups milk**
3	**cups oil**

Cut fish into 4 pieces. Place in large bowl with cold water to cover. Refrigerate, covered, overnight. Drain.

Bring fish and water to cover to boil in 4-quart saucepan. Simmer 30 minutes; drain well. Flake fish.

Beat eggs in large bowl. Stir in onions, red and green peppers, garlic and seasonings. Stir in flour and fish. Gradually stir in enough milk to form thick batter.

Heat oil in large skillet on medium-high heat. Using ¼ cup batter for each cake, cook 3 cakes at a time in hot oil 8 minutes or until brown, turning once. Drain on paper towels; keep warm. Repeat with remaining batter, reheating oil between batches.

Makes 6 servings.

MY MOTHER EUDORA LYLES "DARA" WILLIAMS SAID...

"Keep watch on your words, my darling, for words are wonderful things. They are sweet like fresh honey, but like the bees, they have terrible stings. They can bless like the warm, glad sunshine and brighten a lonely life, but they can cut in the strife of anger, like an open, two-edged sword."

Bettye S. Hunt
Jackson, MS

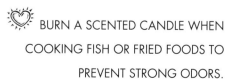 BURN A SCENTED CANDLE WHEN COOKING FISH OR FRIED FOODS TO PREVENT STRONG ODORS.

FRIED CATFISH

1 cup cornmeal
½ cup flour
1 teaspoon salt
½ teaspoon garlic salt
¼ teaspoon onion powder
¼ teaspoon pepper
1 pound boneless catfish fillets, cut into serving pieces
¾ cup shortening
Lemon wedges

Mix cornmeal, flour, salt, garlic salt, onion powder and pepper in paper or plastic bag. Add fish pieces, 3 or 4 at a time; shake to coat.

Melt shortening in large skillet on medium-high heat. Add fish, 2 or 3 pieces at a time; cook 5 minutes on each side or until golden brown and fish flakes easily with fork. Remove from skillet. Drain on paper towels; keep warm. Repeat with remaining fish. Garnish with lemon wedges.

Makes 4 servings.

HERITAGE RECIPE

CATFISH STEW & RICE

3 cups water
2 medium potatoes, diced
1 large onion, chopped
1 tablespoon chopped garlic
½ head small cabbage, chopped
2 large tomatoes, chopped
Salt and pepper
4 fresh boneless catfish fillets, halved
Hot cooked rice

Combine water, potatoes, onion and garlic in large pot. Cook on high heat 15 minutes. Lower heat. Add cabbage, tomatoes, salt and pepper. Cook 10 minutes. Add catfish. Cook 15 minutes. Remove from heat. Serve over rice.

Makes 4 servings.
**Johnny Rivers,
Executive Chef,
Walt DisneyWorld Resorts**

MY MOTHER MARY "MAE FRANCES" BANKS SAID...

"A good name is better than anything else you can choose."

**Gladys B. Brown
Pollocksville, NC**

SPICY SHRIMP & RICE

4 slices Oscar Mayer bacon, cut into pieces
¾ pound medium shrimp, cleaned
1 medium onion, chopped
2 teaspoons Creole seasoning
1 teaspoon dried thyme leaves
¼ teaspoon ground red pepper
1¼ cups chicken broth
1 package (10 ounces) frozen cut okra
1½ cups Minute original or premium rice, uncooked
1 medium tomato, chopped

Cook and stir bacon in large skillet on medium heat until lightly browned. Drain bacon, reserving 2 tablespoons drippings. Add shrimp, onion and seasonings; cook and stir until shrimp turns pink.

Stir in broth and okra. Bring to boil; stirring occasionally to break apart okra. Stir in rice and tomato; cover. Remove from heat. Let stand 5 minutes. Stir.

Makes 4 servings.

MY MOTHER META HUGHES-JONES SAID...

"Whatever goes up, must come down; therefore, it is important to keep your feet and mind planted on solid ground."

Mary Jones-Hills
Bedford Heights, OH

CREOLE RED BEANS & RICE

1 package (16 ounces) dry red beans
2 small smoked ham hocks*
1 large onion, chopped
4 bay leaves
5 cloves garlic, minced
1 teaspoon dried thyme leaves
1 teaspoon crushed red pepper
1 tablespoon salt
½ teaspoon black pepper
1 pound shrimp, cleaned
Hot cooked rice

*Or use smoked beef sausages, cut into 1-inch pieces.

Rinse and soak beans as directed on package.

Bring beans, ham, water to cover, and seasonings to boil in large saucepot. Reduce heat to low; cover and simmer 1 to 1½ hours or until ham and beans are tender, adding water if necessary. Add shrimp; cook 10 minutes. Serve over rice.

Makes 8½ cups.

**Alexis M. Herman,
Assistant to the President,
Diretor of Public Liaison
The White House
Washington, DC**

MY MOTHER ALLONIA HILL RICE SAID...

"Take 10 percent off the top of your allowance and put it in a jar for that rainy day."

**Vera Lee Clanton
San Francisco, CA**

EGGS NEW ORLEANS

¼ **cup (½ stick) Parkay spread stick or butter**
2 **large ripe tomatoes, chopped**
1 **medium pepper, chopped**
1 **medium onion, chopped**
2 **bay leaves**
¼ **teaspoon salt**
⅛ **teaspoon pepper**
½ **cup Stove Top chicken flavor stuffing mix in the canister**
1 **pound cooked crabmeat**
1 **cup (4 ounces) shredded Kraft natural cheddar cheese**
6 **eggs**

Heat oven to 350°F.

Melt spread in large skillet on medium-high heat. Add tomatoes, green pepper, onion, bay leaves, salt and pepper; cook and stir 10 minutes or until tender. Remove bay leaves; discard. Stir in stuffing mix. Spread in 3-quart shallow baking dish. Arrange crabmeat evenly over top; sprinkle with cheese. Press 6 indentations, using back of spoon. Break 1 egg into each indentation. Sprinkle with additional salt, pepper and cheese, if desired.

Bake 5 to 7 minutes or until eggs are set.

Makes 6 servings.

MY MOTHER ELDRA WHEATLAND SAID...

"If you do anything, make sure you do it with your heart."

Patricia Grayson
Bronx, NY

MACARONI & CHEESE WITH WHITE SAUCE

1 cup (4 ounces) elbow macaroni, cooked, drained
4 tablespoons margarine or butter, divided
1 small onion, chopped
2 cups milk
3 tablespoons flour
Salt and pepper
1½ cups shredded sharp cheddar cheese

Heat oven to 325°F.

Melt 1 tablespoon of the margarine in small skillet on medium heat. Add onion; cook and stir until tender.

Mix milk, remaining 3 tablespoons margarine, flour, salt and pepper in medium saucepan. Cook and stir on medium heat until smooth and creamy. Stir in onion.

Place ½ of the macaroni in shallow baking dish; top with ⅓ of the cheese. Repeat layers. Pour white sauce over macaroni mixture. Top with remaining cheese.

Bake 30 minutes or until heated through. Serve hot.

Makes 4 servings.
Nancy Wilson,
Song Stylist

RED BEANS & RICE

5 slices bacon, cut into small pieces
1 small onion, chopped
3 cloves garlic, finely chopped
8 cups water
1 package (16 ounces) dry red beans, rinsed
1 tablespoon salt
2 teaspoons ground cumin
½ teaspoon pepper
Hot cooked rice

Cook and stir bacon, onion and garlic in large saucepot on medium heat until bacon is crisp and onion is tender. Add water, beans, salt, cumin and pepper; bring to boil. Reduce heat to low; cover and simmer 2 to 3 hours or until beans are tender. Add additional water, if necessary. Serve over rice.

Makes 8 servings.

HERITAGE RECIPE

BAKED EGGS & SAUSAGE

8 slices day old bread, cubed
2 pounds bulk sausage, cooked, drained and crumbled
3 cups (12 ounces) shredded Kraft natural cheddar cheese
6 eggs
2½ cups milk
¾ teaspoon dry mustard
1 can (10¾ ounces) condensed cream of mushroom soup
1 can (4 ounces) sliced mushrooms, drained
⅔ cup milk
1 jar (4 ounces) sliced pimientos, drained

Place bread in shallow baking dish. Top with sausage and cheese. Beat eggs in large bowl; stir in 2½ cups milk and mustard. Pour over bread. Mix soup, mushrooms, ⅔ cup milk and pimientos in medium bowl. Spread over top of bread mixture; cover. Refrigerate overnight.

Heat oven to 350°F. Bake 1½ hours or until heated through and center is set.

Makes 10 servings.

MY MOTHER ELOISE WEBB WASHINGTON SAID...

"If you say that you cannot...then you cannot." I have told my daughter the same thing."

Bettye Washington Campbell
Chicago, IL

MY MOTHER ROWENA "SISTER" EVANS MARSHALL SAID...

*T*hrough words and by example, my Mother instilled in me the idea that being a woman should not stop me from doing whatever I wanted to do. She also proved that single mothers can make excellent parents, especially when they have the help and support of the extended family.

Sister (as we called her) was the embodiment of self-reliance. In 1945, at the age of 24, she became co-owner and then owner of a dry cleaners in our hometown of Ft. Lauderdale, Florida. She was the youngest woman in the black community to own a business other than a beauty shop. Before she was 30, she had moved to New York to find a more lucrative means of supporting my three brothers and me, whom she left at home with her parents. We visited her in the summers, and after a few years, two of my brothers went to live with her in the Bronx. I too lived there while I was in graduate school at Columbia University.

In New York, Sister worked in various dry cleaners before eventually opening her own business. She had a reputation for being able to "do whatever a man could do" in the cleaners and at home. She routinely painted our apartment and repaired all kinds of things, including electrical outlets and appliances. From the time she moved to New York in 1950, she kept a chauffeur's license (saying "I can drive a cab if I have to"), even though very few women drove taxis in New York in those days.

In addition to everything else, my mother was a superb cook. Under her tutelage, my three brothers also became excellent cooks. But they all agreed that I was hopeless in the kitchen. I once made my Mother a two-layer birthday cake that was so hard, one of my brothers speared it with a knife and paraded it around the room! He then baked a cake, which was scrumptious.

You will not be surprised to know, then, that I had to call one of my brothers to get one of my Mother's recipes for this book. I didn't dare trust my recollections, because I might have produced something that would be a disgrace to her memory.

Dr. Niara Sudarkasa
President of Lincoln University

CELEBRATING OUR MOTHERS'
VEGETABLES
& SIDE DISHES

COOKOO WITH ONION & TOMATO SAUCE

Sauce:
- 2 tablespoons margarine or butter
- 1 small onion, sliced
- 1 can (16 ounces) whole peeled tomatoes, cut up
- ½ teaspoon salt
  Dash pepper

Cookoo:
- 2 cups water
- 1 package (10 ounces) frozen cut okra
- 1 cup yellow cornmeal
- 1 teaspoon salt

For sauce, melt margarine in medium saucepan on medium heat. Add onion; cook and stir until tender. Add tomatoes, salt and pepper; simmer uncovered 10 minutes, stirring occasionally. Keep warm.

For cookoo, bring water to boil in medium saucepan. Add okra; return to boil. Reduce heat to low; cover and simmer 10 minutes. Gradually stir in cornmeal and salt. Simmer 10 minutes or until thickened, stirring constantly. Serve with sauce.

Makes 6 servings.

FRESH CREAMED CORN

- 6 ears fresh corn
- ¼ cup (½ stick) margarine or butter
- ½ cup milk
- 3 tablespoons sugar
- 1 tablespoon flour
- ½ teaspoon salt
- ⅛ teaspoon pepper

Cut corn from cobs. Melt margarine in medium saucepan on medium heat. Add corn; cook and stir until tender. Add milk, sugar, flour, salt and pepper; cook 5 minutes or until slightly thickened.

Makes 5 servings.

 AN EASY WAY TO REMOVE KERNELS OF SWEET CORN FROM THE COB IS TO USE A SHOE HORN.

FUUL MEDAMES

1 **package (16 ounces) dry pinto beans**
3 **quarts water**
2 **cloves garlic, crushed**
 Salt and pepper
1 **cup olive oil**
⅓ **cup lemon juice**
1 **clove garlic, minced**
 Chopped fresh parsley
 Chopped hard-cooked egg
 Red or yellow onion slices
 Pitted black olives

Rinse and soak beans as directed on package.

Bring beans, water and garlic to boil in large saucepan. Reduce heat to low; cover and simmer 2 hours or until very tender, adding additional water, if necessary.

Mash beans slightly; season to taste with salt and pepper.

Mix oil, lemon juice and minced garlic in small bowl. Stir in salt and pepper, to taste. Serve beans with dressing, parsley, egg, onion and olives.

Makes 8 servings.

GREENS GALORE

6 **cups water**
1½ **pounds smoked ham hocks**
3 **pounds assorted greens (collard, mustard and/or turnip), washed, stems removed and cut into pieces**
1 **teaspoon sugar**
1 **teaspoon salt**
¼ **teaspoon pepper**

Bring water and ham hocks to boil in large saucepot. Reduce heat to low; cover and simmer 1½ hours or until ham is very tender. Remove ham; cool slightly. Remove ham from bones. Return to pot; discard bones.

Add greens, sugar, salt and pepper. Cook on medium heat, stirring and pushing greens down frequently, 30 to 35 minutes or until greens are tender.

Makes 10 servings.

 ALWAYS "BRUISE" YOUR GREENS A LITTLE WHEN WASHING THEM...IT MAKES FOR BETTER TASTE.

GREENS WITH CORNMEAL DUMPLINGS

1 **smoked ham hock**
8 **cups water**
2½ **teaspoons salt, divided**
2 **bunches mustard greens (1 pound each), washed, stems removed**
2 **cups yellow cornmeal**
1 **medium onion, finely chopped**
2 **cups boiling water**

Bring ham hock, 8 cups water and 2 teaspoons of the salt to boil in large saucepot. Reduce heat to low; cover and simmer 1 to 1½ hours or until almost tender. Add greens, bring to boil. Simmer, uncovered, 20 to 30 minutes or until greens are tender-crisp. Remove ham hock; cool slightly. Remove ham from bone. Dice ham. Return to saucepot; discard bone.

Mix cornmeal, remaining ½ teaspoon salt and onion in medium bowl. Gradually mix in 2 cups boiling water until smooth. Drop spoonfuls into boiling greens mixture. Boil 30 minutes. Reduce heat to low; simmer 10 minutes.

Makes 8 servings.

HERITAGE RECIPE

MY MOTHER CECELIA "MISS BAY" GRIFFIN SAID...

"When you have your hand in the lion's mouth, you got to mind how you move it."

Emma B. Broman
New Orleans, LA

COLLARD GREENS WITH SMOKED TURKEY

2 smoked turkey wings or
1 smoked turkey drumstick (about 1¼ pounds)
2 quarts water
3 cloves garlic, crushed
1 large onion, chopped
2 teaspoons salt
2 hot chile peppers, seeded and chopped
2 bunches collard greens (2 pounds each), washed, stems removed and cut into pieces

Bring turkey, water, garlic, onion, salt and peppers to boil in large saucepot. Reduce heat to low; cover and simmer 1 to 1½ hours or until almost tender.

Add greens; return to boil. Simmer, uncovered, 40 to 50 minutes or until greens are tender. Remove turkey; cool slightly. Remove turkey from bones. Return to pot; discard bones. Serve with cornbread.

Makes 8 servings.

HERITAGE RECIPE

FRIED GREEN TOMATOES

1 cup flour
½ cup cornmeal
1 teaspoon salt
¼ teaspoon pepper
¼ teaspoon garlic powder
¼ teaspoon onion powder
¼ teaspoon paprika
¼ teaspoon curry powder
3 medium green tomatoes, cut into ¼-inch slices
¼ cup oil

Mix dry ingredients in large plastic bag. Add tomato slices, 1 or 2 at a time; shake to coat.

Heat oil in large skillet on medium heat. Add tomato slices a few at a time; brown lightly on both sides. Drain on paper towels. Serve hot.

Makes 6 servings.

OKRA & TOMATOES

I said in my second cookbook *Iron Pots and Wooden Spoons* that where okra points its green tip, Africa has passed. Nothing could be truer. The green pods of the okra plant are native to Africa, and, wherever they turn up, Africa has had some influence on the cooking. In many parts of the African-American South and North, African okra frequently turns up in a number of dishes. In some dishes the okra is mixed with corn, one of the staples of the New World larder. In others, it is mixed with both tomatoes and corn. Most of the combinations are hot and spicy with chiles or hot sauce; some are seasoned with a smokey piece of bacon or a ham hock; all are delicious.

Okra and Tomatoes is a simple dish but one that is at home on virtually any table from a summer barbecue to a New Year's buffet. Even the colors of this dish are a part of our history as the red of the tomatoes, the green of the okra, and the the gold of the corn are the colors of many an African flag.

—**Jessica B. Harris**

ONIONS, OKRA, CORN & TOMATOES

½ **pound bacon** 1 **large onion, sliced** 3 **large tomatoes, sliced** 2 **cans (16 ounces each) whole kernel corn, drained** 1 **package (10 ounces) frozen cut okra** ¾ **teaspoon salt** ¼ **teaspoon pepper**	Cook bacon in large saucepan on medium heat until crisp, turning frequently. Drain, reserving 2 table-spoons drippings in saucepan. Heat reserved drippings in saucepan on medium heat. Add onion; cook and stir until tender. Add tomatoes, corn, okra, salt and pepper; cover and simmer 30 minutes, stirring occasionally. Crumble bacon; sprinkle over top just before serving. *Makes 10 servings.*

HERITAGE RECIPE

SUMMER SQUASH & CORN CASSEROLE

1 **pound yellow squash or zucchini, sliced**
2 **tablespoons margarine or butter**
1 **large onion, diced**
1 **small green pepper, diced**
2 **cans (16 ounces each) cream-style corn**
1½ **cups Stove Top cornbread stuffing mix in the canister, divided**
1 **cup (4 ounces) shredded Kraft natural cheddar cheese**
1 **egg, beaten**
1 **teaspoon sugar**
1 **teaspoon seasoned salt**
1 **tablespoon margarine or butter, melted**

Heat oven to 350°F.

Cook squash in enough boiling water to cover in medium saucepan until tender. Drain.

Melt 2 tablespoons margarine in large skillet on medium heat. Add onion and pepper; cook and stir until tender.

Mix squash, onion, pepper, corn, ½ cup of the stuffing mix, cheese, egg, sugar and salt in large bowl. Spoon into 9-inch square baking pan.

Bake 20 minutes. Toss remaining 1 cup stuffing mix with 1 tablespoon melted margarine; sprinkle on casserole. Bake 10 minutes or until bubbly.

Makes 10 servings.

 FOR TENDER CORN ON THE COB, ADD ONE HALF CUP OF MILK AND ONE TEASPOON SUGAR TO THE BOILING WATER BEFORE DROPPING IN THE CORN.

MY MOTHER MAE LIZ POWELL SAID...

"Never leave the house without a dollar in your shoe to get home."

Valorie Powell
Mitchellville, MD

CORN PUDDING

3 **eggs**
2 **cans (17 ounces each) cream-style corn**
2 **cans (17 ounces each) whole kernel corn, drained**
6 **tablespoons flour**
6 **tablespoons margarine or butter, melted**
6 **tablespoons sugar**
1 **cup (4 ounces) shredded Kraft natural cheddar cheese**

Heat oven to 350°F. Grease 3-quart shallow baking dish.

Beat eggs in large bowl. Stir in remaining ingredients. Spoon into prepared baking dish.

Bake 45 minutes or until set.

Makes 8 servings.

CASSAVA MOJO

1½ **pounds cassava, peeled, cut into 2-inch pieces***
1 **medium onion, thinly sliced**
¼ **cup orange juice**
¼ **cup lime juice**
4 **cloves garlic, minced**
1 **teaspoon salt**
½ **cup oil**

*Or use 1 package (24 ounces) frozen peeled cassava; cook as directed on package.

Cook cassava in boiling salted water in 3-quart saucepan 40 minutes or until tender. Drain and return to pan.

Meanwhile, mix onion, juices, garlic and salt in glass or ceramic small bowl. Let stand 20 minutes.

Heat oil in small saucepan over medium heat. Quickly add juice mixture, cook 5 minutes, stirring frequently. Pour over cassava; stir gently to coat well. Serve with roast pork.

Makes 6 servings.

MY MOTHER MATTIE "TENA" BROADNAX SAID...

"People always judge you by your kitchen and bathroom. Keep them clean."

Gwen Jarvis
Cleveland, OH

CREOLE SUCCOTASH & RICE

2 tablespoons oil
1 medium onion, chopped
1 clove garlic, minced
2 cups frozen whole kernel corn
1 cup frozen baby lima beans
1¼ cups chicken broth
1 can (8 ounces) whole tomatoes with liquid, cut up
1½ cups Minute original or premium rice, uncooked
1 teaspoon salt
½ teaspoon dried thyme leaves
¼ teaspoon ground red pepper
2 tablespoons Worcestershire sauce
1 tablespoon white vinegar

Heat oil in large skillet on medium-high heat. Add onion and garlic; cook and stir until lightly browned. Add corn, beans, broth and tomatoes; bring to boil. Stir in rice, salt, thyme, pepper, Worcestershire and vinegar; cover. Remove from heat. Let stand 5 minutes. Stir. Serve hot or chilled.

Makes 6 servings.

 IF YOU HAVE OVER-SALTED VEGETABLES OR SOUP, ADDING A SLICE OF RAW POTATO WILL REMEDY THE SITUATION.

MY MOTHER MAE "MATILDA" J. PEART SAID...
"Always give of yourself, be unselfish and good things will come back to you."

Carolyn Maddox McKie
Suitland, MD

STUFFED ACORN SQUASH RINGS

- **2 medium acorn squash**
- **2 tablespoons Parkay spread stick, melted**
- **1 can (8 ounces) crushed pineapple**
- **Hot water**
- **1 package (6 ounces) Stove Top cornbread stuffing mix**
- **¼ cup (½ stick) Parkay spread stick, cut into pieces**
- **¼ cup chopped pecans, toasted**
- **¼ cup raisins**
- **2 green onions, thinly sliced**
- **1 small carrot, grated**
- **½ teaspoon pepper**

Heat oven to 350°F.

Cut squash crosswise into 1-inch-thick slices. Arrange squash slices in 15x10x1-inch baking pan. Brush with melted spread; cover. Bake 15 minutes.

Drain pineapple, reserving pineapple and juice separately. Add hot water to reserved juice to measure 1½ cups. Stir contents of vegetable/seasoning packet, juice mixture and ¼ cup spread in medium bowl to melt spread. Stir in pineapple, pecans, raisins, green onions, carrot and pepper. Stir in stuffing crumbs just to moisten. Mound stuffing mixture evenly on squash slices.

Bake 20 minutes or until squash is tender.

Makes 8 servings.

MY MOTHER ROSALIE BARRON SAID...

"Even though a bird flies high into the air, he must come down to the ground to gather food to eat."

Helena Johnson
Fontana, CA

STRING BEANS "LA BELLA"

2 tablespoons oil
2 medium onions, chopped
4 cloves garlic, minced
2 cans (16 ounces each) whole peeled tomatoes, cut up
1 can (6 ounces) tomato paste
½ teaspoon dried oregano leaves
¼ teaspoon seasoned salt
⅛ teaspoon pepper
4 cups water
2 pounds green beans
1½ cups (6 ounces) shredded mozzarella cheese
1½ cups (6 ounces) shredded provolone cheese

Heat oil in medium saucepan on medium-high heat. Add onions and garlic; cook and stir until tender. Stir in tomatoes, paste, oregano, salt and pepper. Reduce heat to medium-low; simmer 15 minutes, stirring frequently.

Bring water to boil in 5-quart Dutch oven or saucepot. Add beans; cook, covered, 5 minutes or until crisp-tender. Drain. Spoon small amount tomato mixture into Dutch oven. Top with half of the beans, cheeses and tomato mixture; repeat layers.

Cook, covered, on medium heat until cheeses melt and mixture is heated through.

Makes 12 servings.
Patti LaBelle,
Queen of Rock 'n Soul

MY MOTHER ZEPORAH "SUG" JOHNSON GILLEY SAID...

"You need not tell others what you can do....Do it and let others tell you."

Zeporah Booker
Lexington, MS

SPINACH ARTICHOKE CASSEROLE

3 tablespoons margarine or butter **½ onion, chopped** **1 package (10 ounces) frozen chopped spinach, thawed, drained** **3 eggs, separated** **1 can (16 ounces) artichoke hearts, chopped** **3 slices cooked bacon, crumbled (optional)** **1 tablespoon grated Parmesan cheese**	Melt margarine in large skillet on medium heat. Add onions; cook and stir until tender. Stir in spinach. Add egg yolks; beat until thick. Cool. Beat egg whites with electric mixer in large bowl until stiff peaks form. Gently stir into spinach mixture. Heat oven to 350°F. Grease 1½-quart casserole. Place artichokes in casserole. Top with spinach mixture. Sprinkle with bacon and cheese. Place casserole in larger pan. Fill larger pan with hot water to depth of 1 inch. Bake 40 minutes or until set.

Makes 4 servings.
Nora Hall,
Stacey Hall-Reddick Caterer

MARY'S FRIED CABBAGE & NOODLES

½ cup (1 stick) margarine or butter **1 large onion, chopped** **½ medium cabbage, shredded** **1 carrot, shredded** **1½ teaspoons caraway seed** **½ teaspoon salt** **¼ teaspoon pepper** **6 cups egg noodles, uncooked**	Melt margarine in large skillet on medium heat. Add onion, cabbage and carrot; cook and stir until tender. Stir in caraway seed, salt and pepper. Prepare noodles as directed on package; drain. Stir noodles into cabbage mixture.

Makes 8 servings.

 PUT CINNAMON ON THE CORNER OF THE POT WHEN COOKING ANYTHING WITH A CABBAGE FLAVOR TO REMOVE THE SMELL.

NOLA'S CHEESY MACARONI & CHEESE

1 **package (16 ounces) small shell or elbow macaroni, cooked, drained**
3 **tablespoons Parkay spread stick or butter**
1 **tablespoon flour**
3 **cups milk, divided**
6 **cups (24 ounces) shredded Kraft natural cheddar cheese, divided**
2 **eggs**

Heat oven to 350°F. Place macaroni in 4-quart shallow baking dish.

Melt spread in medium saucepan on medium-low heat. Stir in flour. Gradually stir in 2 cups of the milk; cook until smooth. Add 3 cups of the cheese; cook, stirring constantly until sauce is thickened. Pour over macaroni. Add remaining cheese; stir gently until thoroughly mixed.

Beat eggs in small bowl; stir in remaining 1 cup milk. Slowly pour over top of casserole. Let stand 5 minutes.

Bake 40 minutes or until set and lightly browned. Cool 10 minutes. Cut into squares.

Makes 12 servings.

SAVORY CORN SPOON BREAD

2 **cups hot milk**
3 **tablespoons Parkay spread stick or butter**
2 **cups Stove Top cornbread stuffing mix in the canister**
1 **cup frozen whole kernel corn, thawed**
2 **eggs, beaten**
2 **tablespoons chopped green onions**
2 **teaspoons sugar**

Heat oven to 350°F.

Mix hot milk and spread in 1½-quart casserole until spread is melted. Stir in stuffing mix, corn, eggs, onions and sugar until well blended.

Bake 45 minutes or until knife inserted in center comes out clean.

Makes 4 servings.

 BRUISE GARLIC BY CRUSHING IT WITH A SMALL BOTTLE.

BAKED CHEESE GRITS

4 cups water
½ teaspoon salt
1 cup quick-cooking grits
1 tablespoon flour
1 tablespoon margarine or butter
3 cups (12 ounces) shredded Kraft natural cheddar cheese
2 eggs

Heat oven to 350°F. Grease 1½-quart baking dish.

Bring water and salt to boil in medium saucepan. Slowly add grits, stirring constantly. Reduce heat to low; cook 5 minutes, stirring occasionally. Remove from heat. Mix in flour and margarine. Gradually add cheese, stirring until melted.

Beat eggs in small bowl. Stir small amount of hot grits into eggs. Stirring constantly, slowly pour egg mixture into hot grits. Pour into prepared dish.

Bake 30 to 40 minutes or until firm.

Makes 6 servings.

SOUTHERN RICE CAKES

⅔ cup water
½ teaspoon salt, divided
1 tablespoon Parkay spread stick
⅔ cup Minute original or premium rice, uncooked
1 egg
⅓ cup milk
2 teaspoons grated onion
¼ cup flour
1½ teaspoons baking powder
1 teaspoon sugar
⅛ teaspoon pepper
Log Cabin syrup

Bring water, ¼ teaspoon of the salt, and spread to boil in saucepan. Stir in rice; cover. Remove from heat. Let stand 5 minutes.

Beat egg in small bowl. Stir in milk and onion. Mix into rice. Mix flour, baking powder, sugar, pepper and remaining ¼ teaspoon salt in small bowl. Stir into rice mixture.

Drop by tablespoonfuls onto hot well-greased griddle; brown lightly on both sides. Serve hot with syrup.

Makes 10 rice cakes.

ALABAMA CORN BREAD DRESSING

1 **loaf (16 ounces) white bread, torn into pieces**
2 **cups yellow cornmeal**
1 **cup flour**
2 **teaspoons baking powder**
2 **teaspoons salt**
1 **teaspoon pepper**
1 **teaspoon sugar**
2 **eggs**
4 **cups buttermilk**
½ **cup (1 stick) margarine or butter**
3 **stalks celery, chopped**
2 **large onions, chopped**
1 **cup chicken broth**

Heat oven to 350°F. Line 13x9-inch baking pan with foil extending over edges to form handles; grease foil.

Mix bread, cornmeal, flour, baking powder, salt, pepper and sugar in large bowl. Beat eggs in small bowl. Stir eggs and buttermilk into bread mixture. Spoon into prepared pan.

Bake 45 minutes or until well browned. Lift from pan. Cut into small cubes; place in large bowl. Regrease pan.

Melt margarine in large skillet on medium heat. Add celery and onions; cook and stir until tender. Add to cornbread cubes. Stir in broth. Spoon into prepared baking pan; cover. Bake for 30 minutes or until hot.

Makes 14 cups or enough to stuff a 14 pound turkey.

♥ A FEW DROPS OF LEMON JUICE ADDED TO SIMMERING RICE WILL KEEP THE GRAINS FROM STICKING.

MY MOTHER DARCIE TALLEY SAID...

"You are special...think of yourself as a special person because special people always succeed."

**Ameenah K. McMillan
Iselin, NJ**

CAJUN DIRTY DRESSING

4 slices Oscar
   Mayer bacon, cut
   into small pieces
1 bunch green
   onions, sliced
½ red pepper,
   chopped
2 cloves garlic,
   minced
1 package
   (6 ounces) Stove
   Top cornbread
   stuffing mix
1¾ cups water
1 teaspoon dried
   rosemary leaves
½ teaspoon pepper
½ pound chicken
   livers, chopped
½ cup chopped
   pecans

Cook bacon in large skillet on medium-high heat until crisp, turning frequently. Add green onions, pepper and garlic; cook and stir until tender. Stir in contents of vegetable/seasoning packet, water, rosemary and pepper. Bring to boil; add chicken livers. Reduce heat to low; cover and simmer 5 minutes or until chicken livers are cooked through. Stir in stuffing crumbs and pecans; cover. Remove from heat. Let stand 5 minutes.

Makes 6 servings.

JACK CHEESE PUDDING

¼ cup (½ stick)
   Parkay spread
   stick
1 bunch green
   onions, thinly
   sliced
2 cups milk
1 package
   (6 ounces) Stove
   Top cornbread
   stuffing mix
1 cup (4 ounces)
   shredded Kraft
   natural Monterey
   Jack cheese
2 eggs, beaten
½ teaspoon ground
   red pepper

Heat oven to 400°F. Grease 9-inch square baking pan.

Melt spread in medium saucepan on medium-high heat. Add green onions; cook and stir until tender. Stir in milk and contents of vegetable/seasoning packet. Heat to almost boiling. Add stuffing crumbs; stir just to moisten. Stir in cheese, eggs and pepper. Spread into prepared pan.

Bake 25 minutes or until set.

Makes 6 servings.

TOMATO STUFFING BAKE

2 tablespoons Parkay spread stick
1 bunch green onions, sliced
1 stalk celery, chopped
1 large green pepper, chopped
2 tablespoons firmly packed brown sugar
2 cans (14½ ounces) stewed tomatoes, undrained
⅔ cup half-and-half or milk
1 package (6 ounces) Stove Top cornbread stuffing mix
2 eggs, beaten

Heat oven to 375°F. Grease 2-quart casserole.

Melt spread in medium saucepan on medium-high heat. Add onions, celery and green pepper; cook and stir until tender. Stir in brown sugar. Add tomatoes, half-and-half; cook 5 minutes or until heated through. Remove from heat. Stir in contents of vegetable/seasoning packet. Stir in stuffing mix just to moisten; stir in eggs. Spoon into prepared casserole.

Bake 25 minutes or until set.

Makes 6 servings.

NANNIE'S FRIED POTATOES

6 medium red potatoes
¼ teaspoon dried basil
¼ teaspoon pepper
¾ teaspoon salt
¼ teaspoon seafood seasoning
¼ teaspoon garlic salt
⅓ cup flour
3 tablespoons oil
½ cup sliced onion
½ cup red and yellow peppers

Bring potatoes and water to cover to boil in medium saucepan. Simmer until tender. Drain. Peel potatoes while hot, using slicing tool with ridges. Toss potatoes and seasoning in medium bowl. Add flour; toss.

Heat oil in large skillet. Add potatoes; cook and stir until browned. Push potatoes to side of skillet. Add onion and peppers; cook and stir until tender. Stir potatoes, onion and peppers until blended. Serve at once.

Makes 4 cups.

MARLA'S HASH BROWN SURPRISE

1   package
    (32 ounces)
    frozen chopped
    hash brown
    potatoes, thawed
1   container
    (16 ounces) sour
    cream
2   cups (8 ounces)
    cheddar cheese,
    grated
1   can (10¾ ounces)
    condensed cream
    of chicken soup,
    undiluted
1   cup chopped
    onions
¼   cup (½ stick)
    margarine or
    butter, melted

Heat oven to 375°F.

Mix potatoes, sour cream, cheese, soup, onions and margarine in large bowl. Spoon into 13x9-inch baking pan.

Bake for 1 hour or until brown.

Makes 12 servings.
Marla Gibbs,
Actress

TURNIP POTATO CASSEROLE

4   medium turnips,
    peeled, cubed
3   large potatoes,
    peeled, cubed
½   cup (1 stick)
    margarine or
    butter
1   egg, beaten
2   teaspoons salt
¼   teaspoon pepper

Grease 2-quart baking dish.

Cook turnips and potatoes in boiling water in large saucepan 20 to 25 minutes or until tender. Drain. Mash turnips and potatoes in pan. Stir in margarine, egg, salt and pepper. Spoon into prepared baking dish; cover. Refrigerate 1 hour.

Heat oven to 375°F. Bake casserole 45 minutes or until puffed and brown.

Makes 8 servings.

RANCH POTATO CASSEROLE

2 pounds red potatoes

1½ cups (6 ounces) shredded Kraft natural cheddar cheese, divided

½ cup sour cream

½ cup ranch dressing

5 slices Oscar Mayer bacon, cooked, crumbled

2 tablespoons chopped fresh parsley

1 cup Stove Top chicken flavor stuffing mix in the canister

1 tablespoon Parkay spread stick, melted

Heat oven to 350°F. Grease 9-inch square baking pan.

Cook potatoes in boiling water in large saucepan until tender. Drain. Cool. Cut into 1½-inch cubes.

Mix 1 cup of the cheese, sour cream, dressing, bacon and parsley in medium bowl. Gently stir in potatoes. Spoon into prepared pan. Sprinkle with remaining ½ cup cheese. Toss stuffing mix with melted spread in small bowl. Sprinkle over potatoes.

Bake 30 minutes or until heated through.

Makes 8 servings.

MY MOTHER IRENE "SHEY" WIGGINS SAID...
"God don't like ugly."

Bessie R. Edwards
Brooklyn, NY

SOUTHERN CANDIED SWEET POTATOES

6	**medium sweet potatoes**
½	**cups pecans, coarsely chopped**
1	**cup firmly packed brown sugar**
⅓	**cup pineapple juice**
2	**tablespoons lime juice**
2	**tablespoons margarine or butter, melted**
½	**teaspoon ground cinnamon**

Grease 2½-quart shallow baking dish.

Cook potatoes in boiling water in large saucepan 20 minutes or until tender. Drain; cool until easy to handle. Peel and cut potatoes into ½-inch slices. Place in prepared baking dish. Sprinkle with pecans.

Heat oven to 350°F.

Mix remaining ingredients in small bowl. Pour over potatoes. Bake 30 minutes, spooning glaze over potatoes occasionally.

Makes 8 servings.

BAKED STUFFED YAMS

4	**medium yams or sweet potatoes**
3	**tablespoons half-and-half or milk**
1½	**tablespoons Parkay spread stick**
1½	**tablespoons firmly packed brown sugar**
1	**teaspoon rum extract (optional)**
2	**tablespoons Baker's Angel Flake coconut, toasted (optional)**

Heat oven to 400°F.

Bake yams on oven rack 50 minutes or until tender. Cut off yam tops lengthwise; scoop out centers, leaving a ⅛-inch shell.

Mash yams in medium bowl. Add half-and-half, spread, brown sugar and extract; beat until fluffy. Spoon into shells. Place in shallow baking pan.

Decrease oven temperature to 350°F. Bake 10 minutes or until heated through. Sprinkle with coconut.

Makes 4 servings.

STREUSEL TOPPED SWEET POTATOES

3 cans (16 ounces each) sweet potatoes, drained, mashed
½ cup Log Cabin syrup
1 teaspoon grated orange peel
⅓ cup flour
⅓ cup old-fashioned or quick-cooking oats, uncooked
¼ cup firmly packed brown sugar
¼ teaspoon ground cinnamon
¼ cup (½ stick) Parkay spread stick
¼ cup chopped pecans

Heat oven to 400°F.

Mix potatoes, syrup and peel in large bowl until well blended. Spoon into 2-quart casserole; smooth top.

Mix flour, oats, sugar and cinnamon in medium bowl. Cut in spread until coarse crumbs form. Stir in pecans. Sprinkle over potatoes.

Bake 20 minutes or until heated through.

Makes 8 servings.

♥ A DASH OF BAKING POWDER ADDED TO MASHED POTATOES WILL MAKE THEM FLUFFY AND LIGHT.

MY MOTHER MARJORIE HILL FIELDS SAID...

"Never let 'no' set your limit."

**Dawna Michelle Fields
Mount Vernon, NY**

YELLOW RICE & RAISINS

1½ cups water
2 tablespoons Parkay spread stick
1 teaspoon salt
½ teaspoon ground turmeric
¼ teaspoon ground cinnamon
1½ cups Minute premium or original rice, uncooked
½ cup raisins
1 teaspoon sugar

Bring water, spread, salt, turmeric and cinnamon to boil in medium saucepan. Stir in rice; cover. Remove from heat. Let stand 5 minutes. Stir in raisins and sugar.

Makes 6 servings.

KANSAS CITY GREEN RICE

2 tablespoons Parkay spread stick
2 green onions, chopped
2 cloves garlic, minced
2 cups chicken broth
1 package (10 ounces) frozen chopped spinach, thawed, drained
¼ teaspoon pepper
¼ teaspoon dried thyme leaves
¼ teaspoon dried basil leaves
1½ cups Minute original or premium rice, uncooked

Melt spread in large skillet on medium heat. Add green onions and garlic; cook and stir until tender but not browned.

Add broth, spinach, pepper, thyme and basil. Bring to full boil. Stir in rice. Cover; remove from heat. Let stand 5 minutes. Stir.

Makes 8 servings.

❤ PUT A PINCH OF SUGAR IN ALL YOUR VEGETABLES BEFORE YOU COOK THEM.

HOPPIN' JOHN

On New Year's Day throughout black America, no holiday table would be complete with a steaming dish of Hoppin' John. The mixture of black eye peas, rice, smoked ham hocks and seasonings is as traditional as a New Year's greeting. No one is sure where Hoppin' John originated, but a good guess would seem to be West Africa, as similar dishes are eaten there and wherever Africans have traveled. In fact, some would say that Hoppin' John is black America's answer to the peas and rice of the Caribbean. No one is sure how the dish came to get its name, but there seems to be a suggestion from every cook in the South.

Whatever its origins, Hoppin' John seems to be most at home in South Carolina where Low Country rice is one of the essential ingredients. It spread throughout the South, and today it's a holiday favorite, South and North. On New Year's Day, we eat Hoppin' John for good luck. On all other days of the year, we eat it simply because it's delicious.

Jessica B. Harris

HOPPIN' JOHN - PEAS & PLENTY

2 tablespoons oil
1 smoked ham hock*
1 medium onion, chopped
10 cups water, divided
1 package (16 ounces) dry black eye peas, rinsed
2 teaspoons salt
1 teaspoon dried parsley leaves
1 teaspoon dried thyme leaves
2 cups long-grain rice, uncooked

Or use 1 pound mild or hot Italian sausage, chopped.

Heat oil in large saucepot on medium-high heat. Add ham hocks and onion; cook and stir until browned. Add 8 cups of the water, peas, salt, parsley and thyme; bring to boil. Reduce heat to low; cover and simmer 2½ hours or until tender. Remove ham hocks; cool slightly. Remove ham from bone. Shred ham. Return to pot; discard bone.

Add remaining 2 cups water; bring to boil. Stir in rice. Reduce heat to low; cover. Simmer 20 minutes or until rice is tender, adding additional water for moister consistency, if desired.

Makes 8 servings.

HERITAGE RECIPE

QUICK HOPPIN' JOHN

3 slices Oscar Mayer bacon, cut into small pieces
1 small onion, chopped
1 stalk celery, chopped
1 can (15 ounces) black eye peas, undrained
1 cup water
1 cup Minute original or premium rice, uncooked
2 tablespoons chopped fresh parsley
½ teaspoon dried thyme leaves (optional)

Cook bacon in medium saucepan on medium heat until crisp, stirring frequently. Add onion and celery; cook and stir until lightly browned. Add peas with liquid. Reduce heat; cover and simmer 5 minutes.

Add water; bring to boil. Stir in rice, parsley and thyme; cover. Remove from heat. Let stand 5 minutes. Stir.

Makes 4 servings.

OLD-FASHIONED PINTO BEANS WITH SMOKED TURKEY

1 package (16 ounces) dry pinto beans
6 cups water
1 smoked turkey leg (about 1¼ pounds)
1 small smoked ham hock
3 slices fat back
1 tablespoon salt
½ teaspoon pepper

Rinse and soak beans as directed on package.

Bring water, turkey and ham to boil in large saucepot. Reduce heat to low; cover and simmer 1½ hours or until tender. Add beans, fat back, salt and pepper; cook, covered, about 1½ hours or until beans are tender. Remove turkey and ham; cool slightly. Remove turkey and ham from bones. Return to pot; discard bones.

Makes 10 servings.

CAJUN RICE

4 slices Oscar Mayer bacon, cut into small pieces 1 medium onion, chopped 2 teaspoons chili powder 1 teaspoon dried thyme leaves ¼ teaspoon ground red pepper 1 can (13¾ ounces) chicken broth 1 package (10 ounces) frozen cut okra 1½ cups Minute original or premium rice, uncooked 1 cup canned kidney beans, drained	Cook and stir bacon and onion in large saucepan on medium heat, stirring frequently until bacon is crisp and onion is tender.

Cook and stir bacon and onion in large saucepan on medium heat, stirring frequently until bacon is crisp and onion is tender.

Add chili powder, thyme, pepper, broth and okra; bring to full boil, breaking up okra with spoon. Stir in rice and beans. Cover; remove from heat. Let stand 5 minutes. Stir.

Makes 4 servings.

SKILLET BAKED BEANS

4 slices Oscar Mayer Bacon, cut into small pieces
1 medium green pepper, chopped
1 medium onion, chopped
1 can (28 ounces) pork and beans
½ cup Kraft original barbecue sauce
¼ cup firmly packed brown sugar

Cook bacon in large skillet on medium heat until crisp, stirring frequently. Remove bacon; drain on paper towels. Set aside.

Add pepper and onion to drippings in skillet; cook and stir until tender.

Stir in pork and beans, barbecue sauce and brown sugar; simmer 10 minutes. Top with bacon.

Makes 6 servings.

CHARLESTON RICE

1 can (14½ ounces) stewed tomatoes
1 tablespoon oil
1 cup diced ham
1 large green pepper, finely chopped
2 stalks celery, chopped
4 green onions, sliced
2 cloves garlic, minced
½ teaspoon pepper
2 cups Minute original or premium rice, uncooked
1 tablespoon hot pepper sauce

Drain tomatoes, reserving liquid. Add water to reserved liquid to make 2 cups. Set aside.

Heat oil in large skillet on medium-high heat. Add ham, green pepper, celery, onions and garlic; cook and stir until tender. Stir in tomatoes, reserved liquid and pepper. Bring to boil. Stir in rice and hot sauce. Cover. Remove from heat. Let stand 5 minutes. Stir.

Makes 6 servings.

DIRTY RICE

¼ pound sausage, crumbled
¼ pound chicken livers, finely chopped
1 small onion, finely chopped
1 stalk celery, finely chopped
1 clove garlic, minced
½ teaspoon pepper
¼ teaspoon ground red pepper
1 can (13¾ ounces) chicken broth
1½ cups Minute original or premium rice, uncooked

Brown sausage in large skillet on medium heat. Drain sausage, reserving 1 tablespoon drippings in skillet. Add chicken livers, onion, celery, garlic and peppers; cook and stir until chicken livers are cooked through.

Stir in broth. Bring to boil. Stir in rice; cover. Remove from heat. Let stand 5 minutes. Stir.

Makes 6 servings.

HOT FRUIT CASSEROLE

1 **can (20 ounces) pineapple chunks, drained**
1 **can (16 ounces) apricot halves, drained, sliced**
1 **can (16 ounces) peach slices, drained**
1 **can (16 ounces) pear halves, drained, sliced**
1 **jar (14 ounces) spiced apple rings, drained**
1 **cup sherry**
½ **cup firmly packed brown sugar**
½ **cup (1 stick) margarine or butter**
2 **tablespoons flour**

Place fruit in 2-quart shallow baking dish.

Bring sherry, sugar, margarine and flour to boil in medium saucepan. Pour over fruit; cover. Refrigerate 4 hours or overnight.

Heat oven to 350°F.

Bake 30 minutes or until hot. Serve hot or at room temperature as a side dish or in place of cranberry sauce.

Makes 12 servings.

REMOVE THE ODOR FROM YOUR HANDS AFTER CUTTING ONIONS BY SIMPLY WASHING THEM WITH SALT OR BAKING SODA.

MY MOTHER FLORIDA WADE "FLOYD" BROWN SAID...

"Give service to people. Do something instead of sitting on your bottom thinking about it."

Carneice Brown-White
Denver, CO

MY MOTHER VIOLET TAYLOR SAID...

I come from a long line of hard-working African-Caribbean women. My great-grandmother, Susan, had a restaurant in Trinidad at the turn of the century, and she also started a soda business during that time. When her daughter, my grandmother Rhoda, who had divorced her husband in Trinidad, came to the United States in 1916, she worked as a seamstress, then started a business of her own. Mother, as her children and grandchildren called her, did very well in the numbers business in Harlem during the 1920's and 1930's. Although she built what was spoken of as a "mini-empire" with a man with whom she had a long love relationship, at the end of her life she had no money. Mommy always felt that Mother Rhoda made a tremendous mistake in not having her name on the bank records and the deeds to the many properties that were acquired through the business.

My Mother Violet spoke to me often about this when I was a girl, usually when she was cooking and I was nearby. I remember her saying, "Don't let love make you blind or foolish. Think with your heart and your head. Make sure you have ownership in whatever you and your partner work toward and build together."

Susan L. Taylor
Editor-in-Chief
Essence Magazine

CELEBRATING
OUR
MOTHERS'
DESSERTS

DOROTHY'S DARK FRUITCAKE

Fruit Mixture:
- 2 cups mixed candied fruit
- 1 cup currants
- 1 cup raisins
- ¾ cup chopped walnuts
- ½ cup chopped candied cherries
- ½ cup chopped pitted prunes
- ½ cup mincemeat
- ½ cup rum
- 1 teaspoon almond extract
- 1 teaspoon vanilla

Cake:
- 2¼ cups flour
- 2½ teaspoons baking powder
- ½ teaspoon baking soda
- 1 teaspoon ground cinnamon
- ¼ teaspoon ground allspice
- ¼ teaspoon ground nutmeg
- ¼ teaspoon salt
- ½ cup (1 stick) margarine or butter, softened
- 1 cup sugar
- ½ cup firmly packed dark brown sugar
- 3 eggs
- ½ cup water

For fruit mixture, mix all ingredients in large bowl; cover. Let stand overnight or until liquid is absorbed.

Heat oven to 325°F. Grease 2 (8x4-inch) loaf pans; line bottoms with wax paper.

Mix flour, baking powder, baking soda, spices and salt in medium bowl. Beat margarine and sugars in large bowl with electric mixer on medium speed until light and fluffy. Add eggs, 1 at a time, beating well after each addition. Add flour mixture alternately with water, beating after each addition until smooth. Stir in fruit mixture. Pour into prepared pans.

Bake 1 hour and 45 minutes or until toothpick inserted in center comes out clean. Cool 20 minutes; remove from pans. Cool completely on wire racks. Wrap in plastic wrap or foil. Store in air-tight container.

Makes 2 loaves.

 IF YOUR BROWN SUGAR HAS HARDENED, USE YOUR CHEESE GRATER.

SCRIPTURE CAKE

Down home in rural Arkansas, when my family was all together, we would read the Bible scriptures and get the ingredients together to prepare Scripture Cake at holidays like Thanksgiving and Christmas. Each person would read the verse of the scripture as they brought the ingredients. Then we'd put them together and make the cake. When it was ready, we'd serve it for dessert at the end of the family meal. Preparing Scripture Cake is time-consuming and not easy, but it's a beautiful cake and a beautiful way for a family to read the scripture together.

Armentha Nesbitt
Cleveland, Ohio

TRADITIONAL SCRIPTURE CAKE

1½ **cups flour, divided**
   1 Kings 3:22
2 **teaspoons baking powder**
   Corinthians 5:6
1 **teaspoon ground cinnamon**
½ **teaspoon ground nutmeg**
   1 Kings 10:25
½ **teaspoon salt**
   Leviticus 2:13
¼ **teaspoon ground ginger**
2 **cups sugar**
   Jeremiah 6:10
1 **cup (2 sticks) margarine or butter, softened**
   Judges 5:25
2 **tablespoons honey**
   Proverbs 24:13
6 **eggs, separated**
   Isaiah 10:14
½ **cup milk**
   Genesis 24:13
2 **cups chopped almonds**
   Numbers 17:8
2 **cups chopped dates or figs**
   Nehemiah 3:12
2 **cups raisins**
   1 Samuel 30:12
2 **tablespoons flour**

Heat oven to 300°F. Grease and flour 10-inch tube pan.

Mix 1½ cups flour, baking powder, spices and salt in medium bowl. Beat sugar, margarine and honey in large bowl with electric mixer on medium speed until light and fluffy. Add egg yolks, 1 at a time, beating well after each addition. Add flour mixture alternately with milk, beating after each addition until smooth.

Beat egg whites in another large bowl with electric mixer using clean beaters on high speed until stiff peaks form. Gently stir into batter. Toss almonds, dates, raisins and 2 tablespoons flour in small bowl. Stir into batter. Pour into prepared pan.

Bake 2 hours and 45 minutes or until toothpick inserted into center comes out clean. Cool 10 minutes; loosen from sides of pan with spatula or knife and gently remove cake. Cool completely on wire rack.

Makes 16 servings.

POUND CAKE

Pound Cake is an all-purpose dessert in the African-American world. It can be served hot, fresh from the oven, just plain or with a light dusting of powdered sugar. It can turn up topped with a scoop of ice cream and a dash of freshly made chocolate sauce, or it can even turn up toasted as a leftover from the dessert of the night before. It's the baker's standby.

Originally prepared from a pound of each ingredient (flour, sugar, and so forth), the pound cake had been a kitchen standby in African-American homes for more than a century. Its simplicity goes well with a basic, no frills attitude to everyday desserts.

However, like many things in the African-American world, the pound cake is incredibly versatile. It can be left plain and taken to offer solace to a grieving family, or it can be decorated with birthday candles and transformed into something even more magnificent with the addition of an icing or a filling or both. Dressed up in its Sunday best, the pound cake is the centerpiece of many a dessert table, church tea, or bake sale.

—Jessica B. Harris

SOUR CREAM POUND CAKE

2 cups flour	
1 teaspoon baking powder	
½ teaspoon salt	
1 cup (2 sticks) butter, softened	
1⅔ cups sugar	
5 eggs	
1½ teaspoons vanilla	
½ cup sour cream	

Heat oven to 325°F. Grease 9x5-inch loaf pan.

Mix flour, baking powder and salt in small bowl. Beat butter and sugar in large bowl with electric mixer on medium speed until light and fluffy. Add eggs, 1 at a time, beating well after each addition. Beat in vanilla. Add flour mixture alternately with sour cream, stirring after each addition until smooth. Pour into prepared pan.

Bake 1 hour and 10 minutes or until toothpick inserted in center comes out clean. Cool 10 minutes; remove from pan. Cool completely on wire rack.

Makes 12 servings.

For Lemon-Poppy Seed Pound Cake: Prepare as directed, beating in 1 tablespoon lemon juice, 1 teaspoon grated lemon peel and 3 tablespoons poppy seed with the vanilla. Bake 1 hour and 20 minutes or until toothpick inserted in center comes out clean.

For Coffee & Cream Pound Cake: Prepare as directed, increasing sugar to 2 cups. Mix 4 teaspoons instant Sanka brand 99.7% caffeine free coffee with the vanilla in small cup; add to batter. Continue as directed above.

PUMPKIN PIE CAKE

½ cup (1 stick) margarine or butter, melted
1 package (2-layer size) yellow cake mix
4 eggs, divided
1 can (29 ounces) pumpkin
1½ cups sugar, divided
⅔ cup evaporated milk
½ cup firmly packed brown sugar
1½ teaspoons ground cinnamon
½ cup (1 stick) margarine or butter, softened
½ cup chopped walnuts
Cool Whip whipped topping

Heat oven to 350°F. Grease and flour 13x9-inch baking pan.

Mix melted margarine, cake mix and 1 of the eggs in large bowl. Measure 1 cup cake mix mixture; set aside. Press remaining cake mix mixture onto bottom of prepared pan.

Beat pumpkin, 1 cup of the sugar, milk, brown sugar, cinnamon and remaining 3 eggs in large bowl with electric mixer on medium speed until smooth. Pour into crust-lined pan.

Mix reserved 1 cup cake mix mixture and softened margarine in small bowl. Add walnuts and remaining ½ cup sugar; mix well. Sprinkle over pumpkin mixture.

Bake 1 hour or until knife inserted 1-inch from edge comes out clean. Cool on wire rack. Serve warm or at room temperature with whipped topping.

Makes 16 servings.

CHERRY POUND CAKE

Cake:
- 1 jar (10 ounces) maraschino cherries, divided
- 3¾ cups plus 1 tablespoon flour
- ¼ teaspoon salt
- 1 cup shortening
- ½ cup (1 stick) margarine or butter, softened
- 2 cups sugar
- 6 eggs
- ½ teaspoon vanilla or almond extract
- ¾ cup milk

Frosting:
- 3 ounces cream cheese, softened
- 4 tablespoons (½ stick) margarine or butter, softened
- 2 cups powdered sugar
- 1 teaspoon vanilla or almond extract
- ½ cup chopped nuts (optional)

Heat oven to 325°F. Grease and flour a 9x5-inch loaf pan.

Drain cherries, reserving juice. Reserve half of the cherries and juice for frosting. Slice ½ of the remaining cherries into halves. Toss cherry halves with 1 tablespoon of the flour in small bowl. Chop remaining cherries; set aside.

Mix remaining 3¾ cups flour and salt in medium bowl. Beat shortening, butter and sugar in large bowl with electric mixer on medium speed until light and fluffy. Add eggs, 1 at a time, beating well after each addition. Beat in vanilla. Add flour mixture alternately with milk, beating after each addition until smooth. Gently stir in flour-coated cherry halves. Spoon into prepared pan.

Bake 90 minutes or until a toothpick inserted in center comes out clean. Cool 10 minutes; remove from pan. Cool completely on wire rack.

For frosting, chop reserved cherries. Beat cream cheese, margarine and powdered sugar in medium bowl with electric mixer on medium speed until creamy. Stir in vanilla, chopped cherries, reserved juice and nuts.

Makes 1 loaf.
Dr. Mabel Phifer,
President,
The Black College Satellite Network

RED VELVET CAKE

2½ cups flour
1 teaspoon baking soda
1 teaspoon salt
1 teaspoon cocoa
1½ cups sugar
1½ cups oil
2 eggs
2 bottles (1 ounce each) red food coloring
1 teaspoon vanilla
1 teaspoon vinegar
1 cup buttermilk
Cream Cheese Frosting
½ cup chopped pecans

Heat oven to 350°F. Grease and flour 2 (9-inch) round baking pans.

Mix flour, baking soda, salt and cocoa in medium bowl. Beat sugar and oil in large bowl with electric mixer on medium-high speed until well blended. Add eggs, 1 at a time, beating well after each addition. Beat in food coloring, vanilla and vinegar. Add flour mixture alternately with buttermilk, stirring until smooth after each addition. Pour into prepared pans.

Bake 35 minutes or until toothpick inserted in center comes out clean. Cool 10 minutes; remove from pans. Cool completely on wire racks. Fill and frost cake layers with Cream Cheese Frosting. Sprinkle with nuts.

Makes 12 servings.

Cream Cheese Frosting: Beat 1 package (8 ounces) Philadelphia Brand cream cheese, softened and 1 stick (8 tablespoons) margarine or butter, softened in large bowl with electric mixer on medium speed until smooth. Gradually beat in 1 package (16 ounces) powdered sugar and 1 teaspoon vanilla. If frosting becomes too thick, beat in milk by teaspoonfuls until of spreading consistency.

MY MOTHER ELOISE PERRY SAID...

"Don't follow other people, follow your own mind and you will never go wrong in life."

**Dorothy Grier
Cincinnati, OH**

VANILLA WAFER CAKE

1 cup (2 sticks) margarine or butter, softened
2 cups sugar
6 eggs
½ cup evaporated milk
1 package (12 ounces) vanilla wafer cookies, crushed (3 cups)
1⅓ cups Baker's Angel Flake coconut
1 cup pecans, ground

Heat oven to 350°F. Grease and flour 9-inch tube pan.

Beat butter and sugar in large bowl with electric mixer on medium speed until light and fluffy. Add eggs, 1 at a time, beating well after each addition. Beat in milk. Stir in crumbs, coconut and pecans. Spoon into prepared pan.

Bake 1 hour or until toothpick inserted in center comes out clean. Cool 15 minutes; remove from pan. Cool completely on wire rack.

Makes 12 servings.

TEXAS PECAN CANDY CAKE

1½ cups pitted dates, coarsely chopped
1⅓ cups candied red cherries, quartered
1 cup candied pineapple, coarsely chopped
2 tablespoons flour
4⅓ cups pecans, coarsely chopped
1¼ cups Baker's Angel Flake coconut
1 can (14 ounces) sweetened condensed milk

Heat oven to 250°F. Grease and flour 9-inch tube pan with removable bottom.

Mix dates, cherries and pineapple in large bowl. Sprinkle with flour; toss to coat well. Add pecans and coconut; toss well. Stir in sweetened condensed milk until well blended. Spoon evenly into prepared pan.

Bake 1½ hours or until top appears dry. Cool completely in pan on wire rack. Remove from pan. Store tightly wrapped in foil in refrigerator. Slice chilled cake with a serrated knife.

Makes 32 servings.

HEAVENLY ANGEL CAKE

Cake:
- 14 egg whites, at room temperature
- 1 teaspoon cream of tartar
- Dash salt
- 1¾ cups sugar
- 1½ cups cake flour
- 2 teaspoons vanilla
- 1 teaspoon lemon juice
- ½ teaspoon almond extract

Frosting:
- 1 package (4 ounces) Baker's German sweet chocolate
- 1 tub (8 ounces) Cool Whip chocolate non-dairy whipped topping, thawed

For cake, heat oven to 300°F.

Beat egg whites in large bowl with electric mixer on high speed until foamy. Add cream of tartar and salt; beat until soft peaks form. Gently stir in sugar. Add flour, in 2 additions, gently stirring until blended. Mix in vanilla, lemon juice and almond extract. Spoon batter into ungreased 10-inch tube pan; smooth top.

Bake 1 hour or until toothpick inserted in center comes out clean. Immediately invert pan over funnel. Cool completely. Loosen edges of cake with spatula or knife and gently remove from pan. Cut cake horizontally into 3 layers.

For frosting, finely chop or grate chocolate; reserve 1 tablespoon. Gently stir remaining chocolate into whipped topping in medium bowl. Fill and frost top only of cake layers with whipped topping mixture, leaving sides unfrosted. Sprinkle top with reserved chocolate. Refrigerate until ready to serve. Store leftover cake in refrigerator.

Makes 12 servings.

MY MOTHER OLIVIA O'NEAL "THE GENERAL" DICKENS SAID...

"You are not wealthy so you only have your faith in the Almighty, your word, and reputation. If these don't amount to anything, then you don't amount to anything."

Rose Marie Dickens Swanson
Detroit, MI

WORLD WAR I CAKE

2 cups water
2 cups sugar
1 cup shortening
1 cup raisins
2 teaspoons ground cinnamon
2 teaspoons instant Maxwell House coffee
1 teaspoon ground cloves
½ teaspoon ground nutmeg
¼ teaspoon salt
4 cups sifted flour
2 teaspoons baking soda
1 teaspoon baking powder
1 cup chopped walnuts
Candied cherries (optional)
Walnut halves (optional)

Heat oven to 350°F. Grease 13x9-inch baking pan.

Bring water, sugar, shortening, raisins, cinnamon, coffee, cloves, nutmeg and salt to boil in medium saucepan. Reduce heat to low; simmer 5 minutes. Cool.

Mix flour, baking soda and baking powder in large bowl. Beat in water mixture with electric mixer on low speed. Stir in chopped walnuts. Pour into prepared pan. Arrange cherries and walnut halves over top.

Bake 30 to 35 minutes or until toothpick inserted in center comes out clean. Cool completely in pan on wire rack.

Makes 16 servings.

REMOVE A CAKE FROM A PAN BY PLACING A COLD TOWEL ON THE BOTTOM OF THE PAN...COMES OUT SMOOTH EVERY TIME.

MY MOTHER MAYME VICKS-PHELPS WILLIAMS "SWEETIE" COOPER SAID...

"If you are so smart, tell me what is better than goodness?"

Lucy Cooper Summers
Hartford, CT

FRESH APPLE CAKE

Cake:
- 3 **cups flour**
- 1 **teaspoon baking soda**
- 1 **teaspoon salt**
- 2 **cups sugar**
- 1 **cup oil**
- 3 **eggs**
- 2 **teaspoons vanilla**
- 3 **medium baking apples, peeled, chopped**
- 1 **cup chopped walnuts**

Topping:
- ¼ **cup (½ stick) margarine or butter**
- ½ **cup firmly packed brown sugar**
- ⅓ **cup milk**

Heat oven to 325°F. Grease 13x9-inch baking pan.

For cake, mix flour, baking soda and salt in medium bowl. Mix sugar, oil, eggs and vanilla with wire whisk in large bowl until smooth. Stir in flour mixture. Stir in apples and nuts. Pour into prepared pan.

Bake 1 hour or until golden and toothpick inserted in center comes out clean. Cool in pan on wire rack.

For topping, melt margarine in small saucepan on medium heat. Stir in sugar and milk; bring to boil. Reduce heat to low; simmer 3 minutes. Pierce cake with large fork at ½-inch intervals. Drizzle topping over cake while still warm.

Makes 16 servings.

WHEN PUTTING BATTER INTO A PAN, SPOON OUT THE MIDDLE SECTION AND FILL IN EACH END...THIS WILL MAKE THE CAKE LEVEL AND FLAT.

MY MOTHER FORINE BREWTON "SMILEY" FOWLER SAID...

"Your word is your bond."

Sandra R. Fowler
Alexandria, VA

GINGERBREAD

There were ten of us, and my Mother would make gingerbread in the afternoon; it would just perfume the whole house. She would serve that gingerbread when we'd come home from school. She'd say, "Rest a while; then have your dinner; then get your lessons; then wash up and go to bed." She'd cook the gingerbread in a special pan and cut it into squares. I'd always want the corner piece. It was so nice and crispy.

—Bettye S. Hunt
Jackson, Mississippi

AFTERSCHOOL GINGERBREAD

2½ **cups flour**
1 **teaspoon ground cinnamon**
1 **teaspoon ground ginger**
½ **teaspoon ground allspice**
½ **teaspoon ground nutmeg**
⅔ **cup margarine or butter, softened**
½ **cup sugar**
1 **cup molasses**
2 **eggs**
1 **teaspoon baking soda**
1 **cup boiling water**

Heat oven to 350°F. Grease and flour 9-inch square baking pan.

Mix flour and spices in medium bowl. Beat margarine and sugar in large bowl with electric mixer at medium speed until light and fluffy. Add molasses and eggs; beat until smooth. Gradually add flour mixture; beat until combined. Dissolve baking soda in boiling water. Stir into flour mixture. Pour into prepared pan.

Bake 45 minutes or until toothpick inserted in center comes out clean. Cool completely in pan on wire rack. Cut into squares.

Makes 12 servings.

MY MOTHER CORINNE VALENTINE SAUNDERS SAID...

"There are five senses, but you need a sixth in life...A sense of humor."

Adeline M. Williams
Charlotte, NC

JACKIE'S CHEESECAKE

Crust:
- 1 **cup graham cracker crumbs**
- 3 **tablespoons sugar**
- 3 **tablespoons margarine or butter, melted**

Filling:
- 2 **packages (8 ounces each) Philadelphia Brand cream cheese, softened**
- ¾ **cup sugar**
- ¼ **cup flour**
- 2 **eggs**
- 1 **cup light cream**
- 1½ **teaspoons vanilla**
- 1 **jar (12 ounces) cherry preserves**

Heat oven to 325°F.

For crust, mix crumbs, sugar and margarine in small bowl. Press onto bottom of 9-inch springform pan. Bake 10 minutes. Cool on wire rack.

For filling, beat cream cheese, sugar and flour in large bowl with electric mixer on medium speed until well blended. Add eggs, 1 at a time, beating well after each addition. Beat in cream and vanilla. Pour into prepared pan.

Bake 35 to 45 minutes or until center is almost set. Cool on wire rack. Refrigerate 4 hours or overnight until firm. Run a small knife or spatula around sides of pan to loosen crust; remove sides of pan. Top with preserves.

Makes 10 servings.

WHEN BAKING A CAKE, MAKE SURE ALL INGREDIENTS ARE ROOM TEMPERATURE BEFORE MIXING.

MY GRANDMOTHER VELNER F. DILLARD SAID...

"You are no better than anyone else on this earth and no one is better than you. You must always carry yourself better because you are a child of God."

Daria L. Dillard Stone
Dayton, OH

APPLESAUCE CAKE

2½ cups flour
1½ teaspoons baking soda
1 teaspoon ground cinnamon
½ teaspoon ground cloves
½ teaspoon salt
¼ teaspoon ground ginger
½ cup (1 stick) margarine or butter, softened
2 cups sugar
2 eggs
1½ cups applesauce
1 teaspoon vanilla
1 cup chopped walnuts
½ cup raisins
Powdered sugar

Heat oven to 350°F. Grease and flour 12-cup fluted tube pan or 10-inch tube pan.

Mix flour, baking soda, cinnamon, cloves, salt and ginger in medium bowl. Beat margarine and sugar in large bowl with electric mixer on medium speed until light and fluffy. Add eggs, 1 at a time, beating well after each addition. Beat in applesauce and vanilla. Gradually beat in flour mixture. Stir in raisins. Pour into prepared pan.

Bake 40 minutes or until toothpick inserted in center comes out clean. Cool 15 minutes; remove from pan. Cool completely on wire rack. Sprinkle with powdered sugar.

Makes 12 servings.

BEFORE BAKING, CUT A TRIANGLE IN THE BATTER WITH A KNIFE TO REMOVE AIR BUBBLES.

MY MOTHER EVA WOODS WEBSTER SAID...

"Don't worry about what people say or do to you. Just go on to the end of your row and when they get there, you will already be there."

L. Dianne Webster Madyun
Florence, AL

MOCHA BUTTER FROSTING

¼ **cup milk**
1½ **squares Baker's unsweetened chocolate**
1 **tablespoon instant Maxwell House coffee**
⅓ **cup margarine or butter, softened**
Dash salt
1 **package (16 ounces) powdered sugar, sifted**
½ **teaspoon vanilla**
2 **tablespoons milk**

Heat ¼ cup milk, chocolate and coffee in small saucepan on low heat stirring frequently until chocolate is melted and mixture is smooth and thick.*

Beat margarine, salt and ½ of the sugar in large bowl with electric mixer on medium speed until blended. Add remaining sugar, alternately with chocolate mixture, beating until smooth after each addition. Beat in vanilla and 2 tablespoons milk. If frosting is too thick, beat in additional milk by teaspoonfuls until of spreading consistency.

Makes 2 cups or enough to fill and frost 2 (8-inch) round cake layers or 2 (9-inch) square cake layers.

Note: Recipe may be halved and used to frost 13x9-inch cake.

***Microwave Preparation**: Microwave ¼ cup milk, chocolate and coffee in microwavable bowl on HIGH 1½ minutes or until chocolate is melted and mixture is smooth and thick, stirring frequently. Continue as directed above.

MY MOTHER ANNIE LEE POLK SAID...

"Be honest and true to yourself and do not worry about catering to other people."

Jeannine Ward
Inglewood, CA

MAPLEY CARROT CAKE

2 cups flour
2 teaspoons baking soda
2 teaspoons ground cinnamon
½ teaspoon salt
⅛ teaspoon ground allspice
⅛ teaspoon ground nutmeg
3 eggs
1 cup sugar
¾ cup Log Cabin syrup
¾ cup oil
1 can (8 ounces) crushed pineapple, drained
2½ cups shredded carrots
⅔ cup chopped walnuts
Mapley Cream Cheese Frosting

Heat oven to 350°F. Grease and flour 13x9-inch baking pan.

Mix flour, baking soda, cinnamon, salt, allspice and nutmeg in large bowl. Beat eggs, sugar, syrup and oil in large bowl until well blended. Add flour mixture; beat until blended. Stir in pineapple, carrots and walnuts. Pour into prepared pan.

Bake 45 minutes or until toothpick inserted in center comes out clean. Cool 10 minutes; remove from pan. Cool completely on wire rack. Frost with Mapley Cream Cheese Frosting.

Makes 18 servings.

Mapley Cream Cheese Frosting: Beat 1 package (3 ounces) Philadelphia Brand cream cheese, softened, 3 tablespoons margarine or butter, softened, and 2 tablespoons Log Cabin syrup in medium bowl with electric mixer on medium speed until well blended. Gradually beat in 2 cups powdered sugar until well blended and smooth.

MY MOTHER LOIS RUTH SMITH CYRUS SAID...

"If you want to make it in this world, always treat everyone the way you want to be treated."

Dorothy L. Stevenson
Houston, TX

MAPLEY BERRY SHORTCAKES

- **2 cups sliced strawberries***
- **½ cup Log Cabin syrup, divided**
- **1 cup thawed Cool Whip whipped topping**
- **4 sponge cake dessert shells**

*Or use 1 cup sliced strawberries and 1 cup blueberries.

Mix strawberries and ¼ cup of the syrup in small bowl; cover. Refrigerate at least 2 hours.

Gently stir 2 tablespoons of the syrup and whipped topping in medium bowl. Lightly brush dessert shells with remaining 2 tablespoons syrup. Top with strawberries and whipped topping mixture. Serve immediately.

Makes 4 servings.

APPLE CRANBERRY UPSIDE DOWN CAKE

- **½ cup Log Cabin syrup**
- **¼ cup (½ stick) margarine or butter, melted**
- **1 teaspoon ground cinnamon**
- **2 apples, peeled, cored and sliced**
- **½ cup cranberries**
- **1½ cups flour**
- **2 teaspoons baking powder**
- **¼ teaspoon salt**
- **¼ cup (½ stick) margarine or butter, softened**
- **1 cup sugar**
- **1 egg**
- **1 teaspoon vanilla**
- **¾ cup milk**

Heat oven to 350°F. Grease 9-inch square baking pan.

Mix syrup, melted margarine and cinnamon in prepared pan. Arrange apples over syrup mixture. Sprinkle with cranberries.

Mix flour, baking powder and salt in small bowl. Beat softened margarine and sugar in large bowl with electric mixer on medium speed until light and fluffy. Beat in egg and vanilla. Add flour mixture alternately with milk, beating well after each addition until smooth. Pour over fruit.

Bake 45 to 50 minutes or until toothpick inserted in center comes out clean. Cool 5 minutes. Loosen edges of cake from side of pan; invert onto serving plate.

Makes 10 servings.

SOUTHERN HOT MILK COCONUT CAKE

Cake:
- ½ cup milk
- 1 tablespoon margarine or butter
- 1 cup flour
- 1 teaspoon baking powder
- ½ teaspoon salt
- 1 cup sugar
- 2 eggs

Frosting:
- ⅓ cup firmly packed brown sugar
- 1 tablespoon margarine or butter
- 1⅓ cups Baker's Angel Flake coconut
- ¼ cup chopped pecans
- 2 tablespoons milk

Heat oven to 350°F. Grease 8-inch square baking pan.

For cake, bring ½ cup milk and 1 tablespoon margarine to boil in small saucepan. Remove from heat.

Mix flour, baking powder and salt in small bowl. Beat sugar and eggs in large bowl with electric mixer on medium speed until light and fluffy. Stir in flour mixture and milk mixture just until blended. Spoon into pre-pared pan.

Bake 25 to 30 minutes or until tooth-pick inserted in center comes out clean. Remove from oven. Heat broiler.

For frosting, cook and stir brown sugar and 1 tablespoon margarine in small saucepan over medium heat until melted. Stir in coconut, pecans and 2 tablespoons milk. Spread over cake. Broil 4 minutes or until lightly browned. Cool on wire rack.

Makes 9 servings.

MY MOTHER HELENA G. CUFFINS SAID...

"I love you, and your family loves you, but we may not be with you always. You have to learn to live in this world with other people."

Joyce D. Sowells
San Antonio, TX

POPPY SEED CAKE

Cake:

1 **package (2-layer size) yellow cake mix**
1 **package (4-serving size) Jell-O vanilla flavor cook and serve pudding & pie filling**
4 **eggs**
1 **container (8 ounces) sour cream**
½ **cup Miracle Whip salad dressing**
½ **cup cream sherry or orange juice**
¼ **cup poppy seed**

Glaze:

1 **cup powdered sugar**
1 **tablespoon milk**
1 **tablespoon orange juice**
1 **tablespoon margarine, melted**

Heat oven to 350°F. Grease 12-cup fluted tube pan or 10-inch tube pan.

For cake, beat all ingredients in large bowl with electric mixer on medium speed until well blended. Pour into prepared pan.

Bake 50 minutes or until toothpick inserted in center comes out clean. Cool 10 minutes; remove from pan. Cool completely on wire rack.

For glaze, mix all ingredients in small bowl; drizzle over cake.

Makes 12 servings.

MY MOTHER CALLIE MURPHY LAWRENCE SAID...

"Be kind, understanding and helpful....You must give something back and help someone else. Never hold a grudge because hate and revenge destroy you."

Novell Williams
Orange, NJ

YOGURT CAKE

Cake:
- 2¼ **cups sifted flour**
- ½ **teaspoon baking soda**
- ½ **teaspoon salt**
- 2 **cups sugar**
- 1 **cup (2 sticks) margarine or butter, softened**
- 3 **eggs**
- 1 **container (8 ounces) lemon flavored yogurt**
- 1 **teaspoon grated lemon peel**
- 1 **teaspoon vanilla**

Glaze:
- 1 **cup powdered sugar**
- **Lemon juice**

Heat oven to 325°F. Grease and flour 12-cup fluted tube pan or 10-inch tube pan.

Mix flour, baking soda and salt in medium bowl. Beat sugar and margarine in large bowl with electric mixer on medium speed until light and fluffy. Add eggs, 1 at a time, beating well after each addition. Add flour mixture alternately with yogurt, beating after each addition until smooth. Stir in peel and vanilla. Pour into prepared pan.

Bake 60 to 70 minutes or until toothpick inserted in center comes out clean. Cool 10 minutes; remove from pan. Cool completely on wire rack.

For icing, stir powdered sugar and enough lemon juice in small bowl to make a smooth, pourable glaze. Drizzle over cooled cake.

**Nancy Wilson,
Song Stylist**

IF YOUR CAKE CALLS FOR NUTS, HEAT THEM FIRST IN THE OVEN, THEN DUST WITH FLOUR BEFORE ADDING TO THE BATTER. THEY THEN WON'T SETTLE TO THE BOTTOM OF THE PAN.

MY MOTHER AMANDA "MANDA" COGER-YOUNG SAID...

"Anything that is worth doing is worth doing well."

**Sarah C. Leonard
Charleston, SC**

HEAVENLY CHOCOLATE CAKE

1   **package (2-layer size) chocolate cake mix (<u>not</u> pudding in the mix variety)**
½   **cup unsweetened cocoa**
3   **eggs**
1⅓ **cups water**
1   **cup Miracle Whip salad dressing**

Heat oven to 350°F. Grease and flour 2 (9-inch) round cake pans. Line the bottom of pans with wax paper.

Stir cake mix and cocoa in large mixing bowl; add remaining ingredients. Beat with electric mixer on low speed 30 seconds, scraping bowl frequently. Beat with electric mixer on medium speed 2 minutes.

Pour batter into prepared pans.

Bake 30 to 35 minutes or until toothpick inserted in center comes out clean. Cool 10 minutes; remove from pans. Immediately remove wax paper. Cool completely on wire racks. Fill and frost as desired.

Makes 12 servings.

Variations: Substitute greased and floured 13x9-inch baking pan for 9-inch round cake pans. Bake 35 to 40 minutes or until toothpick inserted in center comes out clean. Cool on wire rack. Do not remove cake from pan to frost. Frost as desired.

Heat oven to 350°F. Grease and flour 3 (9-inch) round cake pans. Line bottom of pans with wax paper. Prepare cake batter as directed. Divide batter between 3 prepared pans. Bake 20 to 23 minutes or until toothpick inserted in center comes out clean. Cool 10 minutes; remove from pans. Immediately remove wax paper. Cool completely on wire racks. Fill and frost as desired.

QUICK CHERRY CREAM TARTS

Pastry for 2-crust 9-inch pie
1 **cup cold milk**
1 **cup sour cream**
¼ **teaspoon almond extract**
1 **package (4-serving size) Jell-O vanilla flavor instant pudding & pie filling**
1 **can (21 ounces) cherry pie filling**
2 **tablespoons slivered almonds, toasted**

Heat oven to 450°F. Invert 8 (6-ounce) custard cups on cookie sheet.

Roll ½ of the pastry to ⅛-inch thickness on lightly floured surface. Cut into 4 (5-inch) circles. Drape over custard cups, pinching to make pleats to fit over cups. Place on baking pan. Repeat with remaining pastry and cups.

Bake 8 to 10 minutes or until golden. Cool completely on wire rack. Carefully lift tart shells off cups.

Stir cold milk, sour cream and almond extract in large bowl. Add pudding mix; beat with wire whisk or electric mixer on lowest speed 2 minutes. Spoon pudding into tart shells. Top with pie filling; sprinkle with almonds. Refrigerate until ready to serve.

Makes 8 servings.

MY MOTHER WILHELMENIA T. VANDERHORST SAID...

"All of your fingers are not even. Look at the middle finger...how 'high' it goes up. Then look at your 'pinky' finger...how short it is. The moral is: No matter how high you go up in life, remember you can always fall back down."

LaVerne V. Robinson
Charleston, SC

MISSISSIPPI MUD NUT SQUARES

Cake:
- 1 **cup (2 sticks) margarine or butter, softened**
- 2 **cups sugar**
- 4 **eggs**
- 3 **squares Baker's unsweetened chocolate, melted**
- 2 **teaspoons vanilla**
- 1½ **cups flour**
- ½ **cup Baker's Angel Flake coconut**
- ½ **cup chopped walnuts**
- 1 **jar (7 ounces) Kraft marshmallow creme**

Frosting:
- ½ **cup (1 stick) margarine or butter, softened**
- 2 **cups powdered sugar**
- 3 **squares Baker's unsweetened chocolate, melted**
- ¼ **cup milk**
- 1 **teaspoon vanilla**
- ¼ **cup finely chopped walnuts**

Heat oven to 350°F. Grease 13x9-inch baking pan.

For cake, beat margarine and sugar in large bowl with electric mixer on medium speed until light and fluffy. Add eggs, 1 at time, beating well after each addition. Beat in chocolate and vanilla. Beat in flour, ½ cup at a time. Stir in coconut and walnuts. Pour into prepared pan.

Bake 30 minutes or until toothpick inserted in center comes out clean. Remove from oven. Immediately spread marshmallow creme over top. Refrigerate until cool.

For frosting, beat margarine and powdered sugar in medium bowl with electric mixer on medium speed until well blended and smooth. Beat in chocolate, milk and vanilla until smooth. Spread over marshmallow creme. Sprinkle with nuts. Cut into 2-inch squares.

Makes 36 servings.

MY MOTHER AMELIA "BABE" SMOAK SAID...

"A good character is better to own than all the worldly riches."

Sara S. Hampton
Charleston, SC

BANANA SPLIT DESSERT

1½ cups graham cracker crumbs
¼ cup sugar
⅓ cup margarine or butter, melted
2 bananas, sliced
1 package (8 ounces) Philadelphia Brand cream cheese, softened
3½ cups cold milk
2 packages (4-serving size) Jell-O vanilla flavor instant pudding & pie filling
1 can (20 ounces) crushed pineapple, drained
1 tub (8 ounces) Cool Whip whipped topping, thawed

Mix graham cracker crumbs, sugar and margarine in 13x9-inch pan. Press evenly onto bottom of pan. Arrange banana slices on crust.

Beat cream cheese in large bowl until smooth. Gradually beat in milk. Add pudding mixes. Beat with electric mixer on low speed 2 minutes or until well blended. Spread evenly over banana slices. Spoon pineapple evenly over pudding mixture. Spread whipped topping over pineapple.

Refrigerate 3 hours or until ready to serve. Garnish with additional banana slices dipped in lemon juices to prevent darkening, if desired.

Makes 15 servings.

♥ CREAM WILL WHIP FASTER AND BETTER IF YOU FIRST CHILL THE CREAM, BEATERS AND BOWL.

MY MOTHER HELEN JONES WOODS SAID...

"Always think about other people before you worry about yourself."
Catherine Liggins Hughes
Washington, DC

MS. ELSIE'S ICE BOX COOKIES

3 cups flour
1½ teaspoons baking soda
1 teaspoon baking powder
½ teaspoon salt
1 cup (2 sticks) margarine or butter, softened
1 package (16 ounces) brown sugar (2¼ cups, firmly packed)
2 eggs
2 teaspoons vanilla
1 cup chopped nuts

Mix flour, baking soda, baking powder and salt in medium bowl. Beat margarine and sugar in large bowl with electric mixer on medium speed until light and fluffy. Add eggs and vanilla; beat until smooth. Gradually add flour mixture, stirring after each addition to form soft dough. Stir in nuts.

Divide dough into 3 equal pieces. Using wax paper or plastic wrap, shape each piece into 8-inch roll. Wrap tightly. Refrigerate 1 hour or overnight until firm.

Heat oven to 350°F. Slice logs into ¼-inch slices. Place on ungreased cookie sheets.

Bake 10 to 12 minutes or until crisp. Remove from cookie sheets. Cool on wire racks.

Makes about 7½ dozen.

MY MOTHER HELEN JANE SCHUYLER ROBINSON SAID...

"No matter how bad you feel you might as well get up and go. You won't feel any better staying at home." Mother did that until she was 105!
Marjorie Robinson MacKerrow
Vallejo, CA

ORANGE GLAZED COOKIE BARS

Cookies:
- **2 eggs**
- **½ cup firmly packed brown sugar**
- **⅓ cup margarine or butter, melted**
- **⅓ cup flour**
- **¼ teaspoon salt**
- **⅛ teaspoon ground nutmeg**
- **2 cups Post Bran'nola lowfat bran granola cereal**
- **½ cup chopped walnuts**
- **½ cup raisins**
- **1 teaspoon grated orange peel**

Glaze:
- **¾ cup powdered sugar**
- **4 teaspoons orange juice**
- **2 teaspoons margarine or butter, melted**
- **¼ teaspoon grated orange peel**

Heat oven to 350°F. Grease 9-inch square baking pan.

For cookies, beat eggs in large bowl until well blended. Beat in sugar and ⅓ cup margarine. Add flour, salt and nutmeg; beat until well blended. Stir in cereal, nuts, raisins and 1 teaspoon orange peel. Spread in prepared pan.

Bake 25 minutes or until lightly browned around edges. Cool in pan on wire rack 10 minutes.

For glaze, mix powdered sugar, orange juice, 2 teaspoons margarine and ¼ teaspoon orange peel in small bowl until smooth. Spread over warm cookies. Cool completely. Cut into bars.

Makes 16.

CHILL DOUGH FIRST, TO KEEP "DROP COOKIES" FROM SPREADING.

"MOTHER BRITT" SAID...

"To a parent, each child is the favorite."

Howard Britt
New York, NY

ONE BOWL BROWNIES

4 squares Baker's unsweetened chocolate
¾ cup (1½ sticks) margarine or butter
2 cups sugar
3 eggs
1 teaspoon vanilla
1 cup flour
1 cup coarsely chopped nuts (optional)

Heat oven to 350°F. Line 13x9-inch baking pan with foil extending over edges to form handles. Grease foil.

Melt chocolate and margarine in heavy 3-quart saucepan on very low heat, stirring constantly. Remove from heat.*

Stir sugar into chocolate until well blended. Mix in eggs and vanilla. Stir in flour and nuts until well blended. Spread in prepared pan.

Bake 30 to 35 minutes or until tooth-pick inserted in center comes out with fudgy crumbs. DO NOT OVER-BAKE. Cool in pan. Lift out of pan onto cutting board. Cut into squares.

Makes 24.

Microwave Preparation: Micro-wave chocolate and margarine in large microwavable bowl on HIGH 2 minutes or until margarine is melted. Stir until chocolate is completely melted. Continue as above.

MY MOTHER MINNIE "MIMI" CROCKETT SAID...

As she was getting me ready for Fisk University, "Never write anything in a letter that you would not like to read in the newspaper the next day."

**Alzeda C. Hacker
Pittsburgh, PA**

NUTTY SHORTBREAD BARS

1 cup (2 sticks) margarine or butter, softened
¾ cup firmly packed brown sugar
1 egg
2 cups flour
1½ cups Post Grape-Nuts brand cereal, divided
½ cup fruit preserves, any variety
1 teaspoon ground cinnamon
1 tablespoon brown sugar

Heat oven to 325°F. Grease and flour 9-inch square baking pan.

Beat margarine, ¾ cup sugar and egg in medium bowl with electric mixer on medium speed until light and fluffy. Stir in flour and 1 cup of the cereal. Spread ½ of the dough evenly into prepared pan. Spread with preserves to within 1 inch of edge. Sprinkle with remaining ½ cup cereal. Carefully spread remaining dough over preserves. Mix cinnamon and 1 tablespoon sugar in small bowl; sprinkle over top.

Bake 45 to 50 minutes or until golden brown. Immediately cut into 16 bars. Cool completely in pan on wire rack.

Makes 16.

♥ WHEN ADDING WATER TO A MIXTURE OR BATTER, NEVER USE COLD WATER.

MY MOTHER JULIA MAE "SMUCK" CARPENTER SAID...

"No matter how you look when you get back home, make sure you look your best when you leave."

Renetta T. Womack-Howard
Lubbock, TX

MAXINE WATERS' TEA CAKES

1½ **cups sugar**
1 **cup (2 sticks) margarine or butter, softened**
2 **eggs**
4 **cups sifted flour**
¾ **teaspoon baking soda**
Dash salt
1½ **teaspoons vanilla**

Heat oven to 350°F. Grease cookie sheets.

Beat sugar and margarine in large bowl with electric mixer on medium speed until light and fluffy. Add eggs, 1 at a time, beating well after each addition. Gradually add flour, beating well after each addition until smooth. Stir in baking soda, salt and vanilla.

Roll dough on lightly floured surface until ½ inch thick, adding additional flour to prevent sticking, if necessary. Cut with floured 2-inch cookie or biscuit cutter. Place on prepared cookie sheets.

Bake 8 to 10 minutes. Sprinkle with sugar. Remove from cookie sheets. Cool on wire racks.

Makes 4 dozen.
Congresswoman Maxine Waters,
State of California

HERITAGE RECIPE

MY MOTHER THELMA JARRETT "THEL" PIGFORD SAID...

"Birds of a feather flock together." She also pointed out: "The most powerful, beautiful birds fly solo...like the eagle."

Evelyn Rose Pigford Acree
Winston-Salem, NC

APPLE DUMPLINGS

6 baking apples, cored (about 3 pounds)
1½ cups firmly packed brown sugar, divided
¼ cup chopped pecans
2 tablespoons margarine or butter, softened
2 teaspoons ground cinnamon
Pastry for 2-crust 9-inch pie
½ cup water

Heat oven to 425°F. Place apples in 13x9-inch baking pan.

Mix ½ cup of the sugar, nuts, margarine and cinnamon in medium bowl. Spoon into each apple.

Roll ½ of the pastry to ⅛-inch thickness. Cut into 3 (7-inch) squares. Repeat with the remaining pastry. Wrap each apple with pastry square; pinch edges to seal.

Heat remaining 1 cup sugar and water in small saucepan on medium heat until sugar dissolves. Pour over dumplings.

Bake 35 to 40 minutes or until tender, basting occasionally with sugar syrup.

Makes 6 servings.

YAM PUFF

¾ cup Post Grape-Nuts brand cereal
½ cup sugar, divided
2 tablespoons margarine or butter, softened
2 cans (16 ounces each) yams, drained, mashed
2 eggs, beaten
2 tablespoons orange juice
½ teaspoon grated orange peel (optional)
2 teaspoons baking powder
½ teaspoon salt

Heat oven to 350°F. Grease 1½-quart shallow baking dish.

Mix cereal, ¼ cup of the sugar and margarine in small bowl. Mix yams, remaining ¼ cup sugar, eggs, juice, peel, baking powder and salt in large bowl. Place ½ of the yam mixture in prepared dish. Sprinkle with ½ of the cereal mixture. Top with remaining yam mixture. Sprinkle with remaining cereal mixture.

Bake 30 minutes or until heated through.

Makes 8 servings.

SWEET POTATO COBBLER

Pastry for 2-crust (9 inch) pie
4 medium sweet potatoes, cooked, peeled and cut into ¼-inch slices
¾ cup sugar
1 teaspoon flour
½ teaspoon ground cinnamon
½ teaspoon ground nutmeg
½ teaspoon ground allspice, divided
½ cup (1 stick) margarine or butter, cut into small pieces
½ cup water
1 tablespoon margarine or butter, melted

Heat oven to 350°F.

Roll ½ of the pastry to 11-inch square on ligtly floured surface. Line 9-inch square baking pan with pastry allowing ½-inch overhang. Arrange potatoes in pastry-lined pan. Sprinkle with sugar, flour, cinnamon, nutmeg and ¼ teaspoon of the allspice. Dot with ½ cup margarine. Pour water over top. Roll remaining pastry to 12-inch square. Cover cobbler with pastry; seal and flute edges. Cut several slits to permit steam to escape. Brush with melted margarine and sprinkle with ¼ teaspoon allspice.

Bake 35 minutes or until golden.

Makes 10 servings.

MY MOTHER DORIS SMITH SAID...

"Respect yourself and others...and never forget where you came from."
Magetta Clue
Cedarhurst, NY

PEACH COBBLER

5 cups sliced peeled peaches
½ cup Log Cabin syrup
¼ cup firmly packed brown sugar
2 tablespoons cornstarch
1 tablespoon lemon juice
½ teaspoon ground cinnamon
¼ teaspoon ground nutmeg
1 cup buttermilk baking mix
2 tablespoons sugar
¼ cup milk

Heat oven to 400°F.

Mix peaches, syrup, sugar, corn-starch, lemon juice, cinnamon and nutmeg in large bowl. Spread evenly in 9-inch square baking pan; cover. Bake 45 minutes.

Stir baking mix, sugar and milk in medium bowl until well blended. Drop by tablespoonfuls onto hot fruit mixture.

Bake, uncovered, 20 minutes or until fruit mixture is bubbly and topping is golden brown. Serve warm with whipped topping, whipped cream or ice cream.

Makes 6 servings.

HERITAGE RECIPE

MY MOTHER LOTTIE GIBBS SAID...

To the nine children in our family. "If you wash the dishes I will give you a sweet kiss." I remember receiving her sweet kiss and her warm caress. I would gladly wash the dishes because I knew my mother was going to spend those precious moments just with me.

Jeni Wallace
Hempstead, NY

FRUIT CRISP

5 cups frozen sliced peaches, thawed
1 tablespoon lemon juice
½ cup Log Cabin syrup
1 teaspoon cornstarch
1 teaspoon ground cinnamon
½ teaspoon ground nutmeg
1 cup flour
1 cup quick-cooking oats
½ cup firmly packed brown sugar
½ cup (1 stick) margarine or butter, cut into small pieces

Heat oven to 350°F.

Toss peaches and lemon juice in large bowl. Add syrup, cornstarch, cinnamon and nutmeg; toss until well blended. Spread evenly in 9-inch square pan. Mix flour, oats, sugar and margarine until crumbly. Sprinkle over peach mixture.

Bake 50 minutes or until topping is browned.

Makes 10 servings.

Raspberry Crisp: Prepare as directed, substituting frozen raspberries for peaches, adding 2 teaspoons sugar to fruit mixture and omitting spices.

Strawberry-Rhubarb Crisp: Prepare as directed, substituting 2½ cups frozen whole strawberries and 2½ cups frozen cut rhubarb for peaches and omitting spices.

MY MOTHER BETTY WOODSON SAID...

"I must have respect for myself as a lady."

Jeanne D. Woodson
Hempstead, NY

CREAMY ORANGE-PINEAPPLE GELATIN DESSERT

1 can (20 ounces) crushed pineapple in syrup, undrained
2 cups boiling water
3 packages (4-serving size) Jell-O brand orange flavor gelatin
1 package (8 ounces) Philadelphia Brand cream cheese, softened
2 cups thawed Cool Whip whipped topping

Drain pineapple, reserving liquid. Add cold water to reserved liquid to measure 2 cups.

Stir boiling water into gelatin in large bowl 2 minutes or until completely dissolved. Stir in measured liquid. Refrigerate 1¼ hours or until slightly thickened (consistency of unbeaten egg whites).

Meanwhile, beat cream cheese in another large bowl with electric mixer on medium speed until smooth. Gradually stir thickened gelatin into cream cheese. Refrigerate 45 minutes or until thickened (spoon drawn through leaves definite impression). Stir in pineapple and whipped topping. Pour into 10-cup mold or bowl.

Refrigerate 4 hours or until firm. Unmold. Garnish as desired.

Makes 12 servings.

Reduced Calorie Dessert: Prepare as directed, substituting 3 packages (4-serving size) Jell-O brand orange flavor sugar free low calorie gelatin, 1 package (8 ounces) Philadelphia Brand neufchatel cheese ⅓ less fat than cream cheese, 1 can (20 ounces) crushed pineapple in unsweetened pineapple juice and 2 cups thawed Cool Whip Lite whipped topping.

DOUBLE STRAWBERRY DELIGHT

2 cups boiling water
1 package (8-serving size) or 2 packages (4-serving size) Jell-O brand strawberry flavor gelatin
1 cup cold water
1 can (21 ounces) strawberry pie filling
1 can (8 ounces) crushed pineapple, undrained
1 package (8 ounces) Philadelphia Brand cream cheese, softened
½ cup sour cream
¼ cup sugar
½ cup chopped nuts

Stir boiling water into gelatin in large bowl 2 minutes or until completely dissolved.

Stir in cold water, pie filling and pineapple. Pour into 9-inch square baking pan. Refrigerate 4 hours or until firm.

Beat cream cheese, sour cream and sugar in small bowl with electric mixer on medium speed until smooth. Spread over gelatin mixture. Sprinkle with nuts.

Refrigerate 2 hours or until firm. Store leftover dessert in refrigerator.

Makes 9 servings.

MY MOTHER JONNIE MAE CLARKE "BRITE" ALLEN SAID...

"Use past mistakes as lessons for the present."

LaTanga Iris Allen
Bronx, NY

FRESH BERRIES VANDEANE

3 cups berries*
4 ounces Philadelphia Brand cream cheese, softened
3 tablespoons milk
1 teaspoon lemon juice
½ cup firmly packed brown sugar

*Suggested berries: raspberries, blueberries or sliced strawberries or a combination.

Place berries in even layer in 9-inch pie plate. Beat cream cheese, milk and lemon juice in small bowl. Spread over berries to within 1 inch of edge. Refrigerate 1 hour.

Heat broiler. Sprinkle sugar over cream cheese mixture. Broil 4 minutes or until sugar is melted. Serve immediately.

Makes 4 servings.

MINCE-PEACH PIE

1 jar (27 ounces) ready-to-use mincemeat
1 can (29 ounces) sliced peaches, drained
Pastry for 2-crust (9 inch) pie
1 tablespoon milk
2 teaspoons sugar
Milk
Sugar

Heat oven to 375°F.

Mix peaches and mincemeat in medium bowl.

Roll ½ of the pastry to 11-inch circle on lightly floured surface. Line 9-inch pie plate with pastry allowing ½-inch overhang. Fill with peach mixture. Roll remaining pastry to 12-inch circle. Cover pie with pastry; seal and flute edge. Cut several slits to permit steam to escape. Brush with milk and sprinkle with sugar.

Bake 45 minutes or until filling is bubbling. Cover edges of crust with foil after 30 minutes, if they become too brown. Cool on wire rack.

Makes 8 servings.

CARIBBEAN FUDGE NUT PIE

1 package
(8 squares)
Baker's semi-
sweet chocolate
¼ cup (½ stick)
margarine or
butter, softened
¾ cup firmly packed
brown sugar
3 eggs
2 teaspoons instant
Maxwell House
coffee
1 teaspoon rum
extract*
1 teaspoon vanilla
extract
¼ cup flour
1 cup chopped
walnuts
1 unbaked pastry
shell (9 inch)
½ cup walnut
halves or pieces

*Or use 1 tablespoon
dark rum.*

Heat oven to 375°F.

Place chocolate in heavy saucepan on very low heat; stir constantly until just melted. Remove from heat.

Beat margarine and sugar in large bowl with electric mixer on medium speed until light and fluffy. Add eggs, 1 at a time, beating well after each addition. Add chocolate, coffee, vanilla and rum extract; mix well. Stir in flour and chopped walnuts. Pour into pastry shell. Decorate top of pie with walnut halves.

Bake in lower third of oven 25 minutes. Cool on wire rack.

Refrigerate at least 1 hour or until ready to serve. Top with whipped cream or ice cream.

Makes 10 servings.

Microwave Preparation: Microwave chocolate in microwavable bowl on HIGH 2 minutes or until almost melted, stirring halfway through heating time. Remove from oven. Stir until completely melted. Continue as directed above.

 PLACE A COOKIE SHEET OR PAN UNDER PIES WHILE BAKING TO ASSURE THE BOTTOM CRUST WILL BROWN.

MY MOTHER HARRIET JOHNSON "HATTIE" POUSSAINT SAID...

"Always try to be a good boy."

**Alvin F. Poussaint, M.D.
Boston, MA**

CREAMY LEMON MERINGUE PIE

Filling:
- 1 **package (2.9 ounces) Jell-O lemon flavor cook and serve pudding & pie filling**
- 1 **can (12 ounces) evaporated milk**
- ¾ **cup water**
- ½ **cup sugar**
- 3 **egg yolks**
- 1 **tablespoon vanilla**
- 1 **baked pastry shell (9 inch), cooled**

Topping:
- 3 **egg whites**
- ⅔ **cup sugar**

Heat oven to 350°F.

For filling, stir pudding mix, milk, water, ½ cup sugar, egg yolks and vanilla in medium saucepan. Stirring constantly, cook on medium heat until mixture comes to full boil. Remove from heat. Pour into pastry shell.

For topping, beat egg whites in large bowl with electric mixer on high speed until foamy. Gradually add ⅔ cup sugar, beating until stiff peaks form. Spread over filling, sealing to edge of crust.

Bake 7 to 10 minutes or until meringue is lightly browned. Cool at room temperature at least 4 hours before serving. Store leftover pie in refrigerator.

Makes 8 servings.

♡ WHEN BEATING UP EGG WHITES FOR MERINGUE, MAKE ABSOLUTELY SURE THE BOWL AND BEATERS ARE DRY...AND THERE IS NOT ONE SPECK OF YELLOW YOLK OR IT WILL BE RUINED.

MY MOTHER HELEN IRENE "MADEAR" CHAVIS SAID...

"Good things don't last forever."

Letitia "Tish" Winfield
Silver Spring, MD

CALIFORNIA CUSTARD PIE

2 eggs
1¼ cups sugar, divided
1½ teaspoons vanilla
2 tablespoons cornstarch
1½ teaspoons flour
2¼ cups milk, divided
¾ cup half-and-half
3 tablespoons unsalted butter
½ cup shredded coconut
½ cup slivered almonds, toasted
1 baked pastry shell (9 inch), cooled
Whipped cream
Toasted coconut

Beat eggs in medium bowl with wire whisk 1 minute. Mix in ½ cup of the sugar and vanilla. Add cornstarch and flour; beat until smooth. Gradually stir in ¾ cup of the milk until well blended.

Place remaining 1½ cups milk and half-and-half in large saucepan. Add remaining ¾ cup sugar; do not stir. Bring to boil on medium heat. Slowly beat in egg mixture with wire whisk. Stirring constantly, bring to boil. Cook and stir 30 seconds. Pour custard into medium bowl. Stir in butter until melted.

Mix coconut and toasted almonds in small bowl. Stir into custard. Pour into pie shell. Cover with plastic wrap.

Refrigerate 3 hours or until ready to serve. Garnish with whipped cream and toasted coconut.

Makes 8 servings.
Dionne Warwick,
Entertainer

MY MOTHER HESTER ELLINGTON OLIVER SAID...

"The world is wise and getting wiser all the time. You must prepare yourself and always be ready for change."

Bobbie J. Oliver Williams
West Covina, CA

MOCHA-ALMOND PIE

2 squares Baker's unsweetened chocolate
2 squares Baker's semi-sweet chocolate
½ cup (1 stick) margarine or butter
1 tablespoon instant Maxwell House coffee
1 cup sugar
¼ cup light corn syrup
3 eggs
2 tablespoons sour cream
1 teaspoon vanilla
1 unbaked pastry shell (9 inch)
½ cup sliced almonds

Heat oven to 350°F.

Heat chocolates, margarine and coffee in heavy 2-quart saucepan on very low heat, stirring constantly until melted. Remove from heat.

Stir in sugar and corn syrup. Beat in eggs, sour cream and vanilla. Pour into pastry shell. Sprinkle with almonds. Bake 45 minutes or until knife inserted 1 inch from center comes out clean. Cool on wire rack.

Makes 8 servings.

Microwave Preparation: Microwave chocolates, margarine and coffee in large microwavable bowl on HIGH 2 minutes or until margarine is melted. Stir until chocolate is completely melted. Continue as directed above.

A TEASPOON OF VINEGAR IN THE WATER USED TO MAKE PIE CRUST WILL MAKE THE CRUST MUCH FLAKIER.

MY MOTHER MARGURITE "MARGIE" MORRIS WATTS SAID...

"Never proceed to eat in front of an unexpected guest when there is not enough food to go around." If you insisted on eating in their presence, then it was customary to invite them unconditionally to eat and to share. With this in mind, I always prepare enough to share.

Barbara Watts Maxwell
Edison, NJ

CREAMY COFFEE PIE

1 **cup cold milk**
1 **package (4-serving size) Jell-O vanilla flavor instant pudding & pie filling**
1 **tablespoon instant Maxwell House coffee**
1 **tub (8 ounces) Cool Whip whipped topping, thawed, divided**
2 **tablespoons Irish whiskey (optional)**
1 **graham cracker or chocolate wafer crumb crust (9 inch)**

Pour milk into medium bowl. Add pudding mix and coffee. Beat with wire whisk 2 minutes. Gently stir in 1½ cups of the whipped topping and whiskey. Spoon into crust.

Freeze 2 hours or until firm. Place pie in refrigerator 30 minutes before serving to soften. Top with remaining whipped topping. Store leftover pie in refrigerator.

Makes 8 servings.

PYI PIE

1 **tub (12 ounces) Cool Whip whipped topping, thawed**
1 **can (6 ounces) frozen lemonade or limeade concentrate, thawed**
1 **can (14 ounces) sweetened condensed milk**
1 **graham cracker crumb crust (9 inch)**
¼ **cup chopped nuts**

Stir whipped topping, concentrate and milk in large bowl. Spoon into crust. Sprinkle with nuts.

Freeze 4 hours or overnight.

Makes 8 servings.

MARY MCLEOD BETHUNE'S SWEET POTATO PIE

1 **cup (2 sticks) margarine or butter, softened**
½ **cup sugar**
½ **cup firmly packed brown sugar**
½ **teaspoon salt**
¼ **teaspoon ground nutmeg**
9 **medium sweet potatoes or yams (4 pounds), cooked, peeled and mashed**
3 **eggs, beaten**
2 **cups milk**
1 **tablespoon vanilla**
3 **unbaked pastry shells (9 inch)**

Heat oven to 350°F.

Beat margarine, sugars, salt and nutmeg in large bowl with electric mixer on medium speed until creamy. Add sweet potatoes; beat until well blended. Beat in eggs. Gradually beat in milk and vanilla. Pour filling into pastry shells, using about 4 cups in each shell.

Bake 50 to 60 minutes or until set. Cool completely on wire racks. Refrigerate until ready to serve. Store leftover pie in refrigerator.

Makes 3 (9-inch) pies.

Pudding Dessert Variation: Pour prepared filling in greased 3-quart baking dish. Bake 1 hour or until set. Sprinkle with 2 cups miniature marshmallows. Bake 5 to 10 minutes or until marshmallows are lightly browned.

from Dr. Dorothy I. Height, President/CEO, National Council of Negro Women, Inc.

When our founder, Mary McLeod Bethune, needed money in 1904 to keep the school doors open she baked and sold sweet potato pies. This is her recipe.

HERITAGE RECIPE

MY MOTHER FANNIE B. HEIGHT SAID...

"No matter what happens, you have to hold yourself together."

Dr. Dorothy Irene Height
President & CEO, National Council of Negro Women, Inc.
Washington, DC

SWEET POTATO PIE

2 eggs, beaten
2 cups mashed cooked sweet potatoes
½ cup firmly packed brown sugar
¼ cup sugar
1½ tablespoons margarine or butter, softened
1½ teaspoons ground cinnamon
½ teaspoon ground ginger
½ teaspoon salt
¼ teaspoon ground allspice
¼ teaspoon ground cloves
¼ teaspoon ground nutmeg
1 can (12 ounces) evaporated milk
1 tablespoon flour
1 unbaked pastry shell (9 inch)

Heat oven to 425°F.

Mix eggs, potatoes, sugars, margarine and spices in large bowl. Gradually beat in milk; mix thoroughly. Stir in flour until well blended. Pour into pastry shell.

Bake 20 minutes. Reduce oven temperature to 350°F. Bake 30 to 35 minutes or until set and knife inserted in center comes out clean.

Makes 8 servings.
**Dr. Niara Sudarkasa,
President, Lincoln University**

💟 ALWAYS MAKE A PIE CRUST WITH ICE WATER TO KEEP IT FROM STICKING.

MY MOTHER CAROLYN L. WEAVER SAID...

"The eagle flies higher than any bird, but he must come down to eat. The success you are capable of attaining cannot be measured, but never forget where you came from or the people you met along the way. Those experiences are nourishing to the soul."

**Princess Weaver
Burke, VA**

BOTTOMLESS APPLE PIE

⅓ **cup Log Cabin syrup**
⅓ **cup firmly packed brown sugar**
2 **tablespoons cornstarch**
1 **teaspoon ground cinnamon**
¼ **teaspoon ground nutmeg**
7 **medium apples peeled, cored and sliced (about 7 cups)**
⅓ **cup raisins**
1 **tablespoon margarine or butter**
 Pastry for 1-crust (9 inch) pie

Heat oven to 425°F.

Mix syrup, sugar, cornstarch, cinnamon and nutmeg in large bowl. Add apples and raisins; toss to coat. Place apple mixture in 9-inch square baking pan. Dot with margarine.

Roll pastry on lightly floured surface to 9-inch square. Cover fruit with pastry. Cut several slits to permit steam to escape.

Bake 40 to 45 minutes or until filling is bubbling and pastry is lightly browned.

Makes 10 servings.

IF YOU HAVE MORE HEAVY CREAM THAN NEEDED IN A RECIPE, WHIP IT...THEN DROP SPOONFULS ONTO ALUMINUM FOIL AND FREEZE. ONCE FROZEN, STORE IN FREEZER BAGS AND USE FOR GARNISHING DESSERTS.

MY MOTHER JOAN ODOM SAID...

"You are the richest person in the world if you are loved and have at least one true friend."

Joan Odom
Brooklyn, NY

FRIED FRUIT PIES

2 packages
(6 ounces each)
dried apricots
½ cup sugar
1 tablespoon
margarine or
butter
½ teaspoon ground
cinnamon
1 package
(15 ounces)
refrigerated pie
crust
½ cup oil
Powdered sugar

Bring apricots and enough water to cover to boil in small saucepan. Reduce heat to low; cook 30 minutes or until tender. Drain, reserving 3 tablespoons liquid.

Place apricots and reserved liquid in food processor container fitted with steel blade; cover. Process until smooth. Add sugar, margarine and cinnamon; process until blended.

Roll 1 of the crusts on lightly floured surface to 15-inch circle. Cut into 6 (4-inch) squares, trimming sides so they are straight. Place 1 tablespoon apricot mixture in center of each square. Fold each square in half to form triangle. Press fork dipped in flour onto edges to seal. Poke tops with fork to permit steam to escape. Repeat with remaining crust and apricot mixture.

Heat oil in large skillet on medium-high heat. Add triangles, a few at a time. Cook 2 to 3 minutes on each side or until golden brown. Drain on paper towels. Sprinkle with powdered sugar.

Makes 12.

MY MOTHER ANNIE JANE TOWNSEND LAMBERT SAID...

"You will be judged by the company you keep so choose your friends wisely."

Vivian E. Howard
Washington, DC

CHOCOLATE PECAN PIE

1 cup Log Cabin syrup
¾ cup sugar
3 tablespoons margarine or butter
2 squares Baker's unsweetened chocolate
3 eggs
1 teaspoon vanilla
1½ cups coarsely chopped pecans or pecan halves
1 unbaked pastry shell (9 inch)

Heat oven to 375°F.

Bring syrup, sugar and margarine to boil in small saucepan. Reduce heat to low; simmer 5 minutes, stirring occasionally. Remove from heat. Add chocolate; stir until melted and smooth. Cool slightly. Beat eggs and vanilla in large bowl. Add small amount hot chocolate mixture to eggs, stirring constantly. Stir in remaining chocolate mixture. Stir in nuts. Pour into pastry shell.

Bake 45 to 50 minutes or until filling is completely puffed across top. Cool on wire rack.

Makes 8 servings.

For Coffee Chocolate Pecan Pie: Prepare as directed, adding 1 tablespoon instant Maxwell House coffee to corn syrup mixture.

ARROZ CON DULCE

2 cans (12 ounces each) evaporated milk
1 can (15 ounces) cream of coconut
2 cups Minute original or premium rice, uncooked
½ cup raisins
1 teaspoon salt
½ teaspoon ground cinnamon
2 teaspoons vanilla

Bring milk, cream of coconut, rice, raisins, salt and cinnamon to boil in medium saucepan on medium heat, stirring frequently. Remove from heat; cool slightly. Stir in vanilla. Let stand, stirring occasionally, until thickened. Serve warm or chilled.

Makes 8 servings.

BREAD PUDDING

8 slices stale white bread, cut into ¾-inch cubes
3 tablespoons margarine or butter, melted
3 eggs
3½ cups milk
¾ cup sugar
½ cup raisins
1 teaspoon ground cinnamon
1 teaspoon vanilla
½ teaspoon ground nutmeg
½ teaspoon salt

Heat oven to 325°F.

Toss bread and margarine in greased 2-quart casserole. Beat eggs in large bowl; stir in remaining ingredients. Pour over bread; cover. Let stand 10 minutes.

Bake 30 minutes; uncover. Bake 30 minutes or until center is set. Serve warm.

Makes 8 servings.

COCONUT PUDDING

3 tablespoons sugar
3 tablespoons cornstarch
2 cups coconut milk, divided
¼ teaspoon salt

Mix sugar and cornstarch in small bowl. Stir in ½ cup of the coconut milk and salt until blended.

Heat remaining 1½ cups coconut milk in medium saucepan on low heat. DO NOT BOIL. Stir in cornstarch mixture. Cook and stir until thickened.

Pour into 8-inch square dish. Refrigerate until firm. Cut into squares. Serve cold.

Makes 4 servings.
**Anna Marie Horsford,
Television Star**

 SMOOTHLY CUT BAKED MERINGUE WITH A KNIFE COATED WITH BUTTER.

MAPLEY SWEET POTATO-BANANA PUDDING

2 cups mashed cooked sweet potatoes
¾ cup mashed ripe banana*
1½ cups heavy cream
½ cup Log Cabin syrup
2 eggs, beaten
½ teaspoon ground cinnamon
¼ teaspoon ground nutmeg
¼ cup flour
¼ cup quick-cooking or old-fashioned oats, uncooked
2 tablespoons brown sugar
2 tablespoons margarine or butter
2 tablespoons chopped pecans

*If bananas are underripe, add 2 tablespoons brown sugar to the sweet potato mixture ingredients.

Heat oven to 350°F. Grease 1½-quart casserole.

Mix sweet potatoes and banana in medium bowl. Stir in cream, syrup, eggs, cinnamon and nutmeg. Pour into prepared casserole.

Mix flour, oats and sugar in small bowl; add margarine and mix until crumbly. Stir in nuts. Sprinkle over sweet potato mixture.

Bake 40 to 45 minutes or until center is firm and top is golden. Serve warm.

Makes 8 servings.

MY MOTHER MABEL "MABE" BROWN SAID...

"Never wake up to a dirty house....It is better to get a clean start on each day."

John T. Brown
Wayne, NY

SOUTHERN BANANA PUDDING

2 packages (4-serving size) Jell-O vanilla or banana cream flavor cook and serve pudding & pie filling
4½ cups milk
3 egg yolks, beaten
42 round vanilla wafer cookies (½ of a 12 ounce package)
2 large bananas, sliced
3 egg whites
Dash salt
⅓ cup sugar

Heat oven to 350°F.

Stir pudding mix into milk in medium saucepan. Add egg yolks. Stirring constantly, cook on medium heat until mixture comes to full boil. Remove from heat.

Arrange layer of cookies on bottom and up sides of 2-quart baking dish. Top with ½ of the banana slices; top with ⅓ of the pudding. Repeat layers, ending with pudding.

Beat egg whites and salt in medium bowl with electric mixer on high speed until foamy. Gradually add sugar, beating until stiff peaks form. Spoon lightly onto pudding, sealing edges well.

Bake 10 to 15 minutes or until meringue is lightly browned. Cool on wire rack. Serve warm or refrigerate, if desired. Before serving, garnish with additional banana slices dipped in lemon juice to prevent darkening, if desired.

Makes 8 servings.

MY MOTHER MARTHA DELANEY "PETIE" BELL SAID...

"Don't ever roll in the gutter for anyone....Wash and iron your one dress, put it on....Eat your bread....Drink your water, wipe your mouth and lift your head high as you walk out the door."

**Marjorie D. Ball
Cincinnati, OH**

PUFF PUDDING

½ cup (1 stick) margarine or butter, softened
1 cup sugar
2 teaspoons grated lemon peel
4 egg yolks
¼ cup lemon juice
¼ cup flour
½ cup Post Grape-Nuts brand cereal
2 cups milk
4 egg whites, stiffly beaten

Heat oven to 350°F. Grease 2-quart baking dish.

Beat margarine, sugar and lemon peel in large bowl with electric mixer on medium speed until light and fluffy. Beat in egg yolks. Stir in lemon juice, flour, cereal and milk. (Mixture will look curdled.) Pour into prepared dish. Place baking dish in another larger pan; fill larger pan with hot water to depth of 1 inch.

Bake 1 hour and 15 minutes or until top is golden brown and begins to pull away from side of dish. Serve warm or cold with cream or prepared whipped topping.

Makes 10 servings.

For individual puddings: Pour mixture into 10 (6-ounce) custard cups. Place custard cups in another pan; fill larger pan with hot water to a depth of 1 inch. Bake 40 minutes or until tops are golden brown and begin to pull away from sides of cups.

MY MOTHER ELLOYD MOORE SAID...

"A bad influence will wear off on you before a good one."

Veronica Cumberland
Pearl, MS

BREAD PUDDING WITH APPLE-RAISIN SAUCE

10 slices whole wheat bread
1 egg
3 egg whites
1½ cups milk
¼ cup sugar
¼ cup firmly packed brown sugar
1 teaspoon vanilla
2 teaspoons sugar
½ teaspoon ground cinnamon
½ teaspoon ground nutmeg
¼ teaspoon cloves
Apple-Raisin Sauce

Heat oven to 350°F. Spray 9x13-inch baking dish with no stick cooking spray.

Overlap bread slices like shingles in 2 rows in prepared baking dish.

Beat egg, egg whites, milk, ¼ cup sugar, brown sugar and vanilla in medium bowl. Pour over bread slices. Stir 2 teaspoons sugar, cinnamon, nutmeg and cloves in small bowl. Sprinkle over bread slices.

Bake 25 to 30 minutes, until browned and top is firm to touch. Serve warm with Apple-Raisin Sauce or at room temperature.

Apple Raisin Sauce: Stir 1¼ cups apple juice, ½ cup apple butter, 2 tablespoons molasses, ½ cup raisins, ½ teaspoon grated orange peel (optional) and ¼ teaspoon *each* ground cinnamon and nutmeg in medium saucepan. Bring to boil; reduce heat to low and simmer 5 minutes. Makes 2 cups.

**Johnny Rivers,
Executive Chef,
Walt Disney World Resort**

MY GRANDMOTHER MOLLY GORDY HADLEY SAID...

"All you need is a willing mind."

**Nettie D. Hailes
Washington, DC**

SWEET POTATO PUDDING

2 cups grated raw sweet potato
1 cup milk
1 cup sugar
2 eggs, slightly beaten
2 tablespoons margarine or butter, melted
1 teaspoon ground cinnamon
¼ teaspoon ground nutmeg
¼ teaspoon salt

Heat oven to 350°F. Grease 1½-quart casserole.

Mix all ingredients in a large bowl. Pour into prepared casserole.

Bake 1 hour or until center is firm. Serve warm.

Makes 8 servings.

PECAN PRALINES

2 cups sugar
2 cups pecan halves
¾ cup buttermilk
2 tablespoons butter
⅛ teaspoon salt
¾ teaspoon baking soda

Mix sugar, pecans, buttermilk, butter and salt in large heavy saucepan. Cook and stir on low heat until sugar dissolves. Cover. Cook 2 minutes on medium heat or until sugar crystals on side of pan are dissolved. Remove cover. Stirring constantly, cook until temperature on candy thermometer reaches 236°F or small amount of mixture forms a soft ball when dropped in very cold water. Remove from heat. Stir in baking soda.

Stir 4 to 5 minutes or until mixture begins to harden. Drop tablespoonfuls onto greased waxed paper. Cool until firm.

Makes 2 to 2½ dozen.

PEANUT CANDIES

Peanuts, although not originally from Africa, have been embraced by the African-American with a vengeance! After all, we are the people who gave the world George Washington Carver, and our culinary uses of the peanut are legion. We are also a people known for our sweet tooth. The result is a hemisphere-wide selection of peanut candies including such delights as peanut patties, peanut chews, and peanut brittle. Most of us haven't tasted homemade peanut brittle in a while, if at all. We're resigned to the almost-there taste of the store-bought variety. However, those of us who have made our own peanut brittle know the fun of preparation, the crunch of home-roasted peanuts, and the sweet savor of caramelized sugar. We know that there's nothing to match the taste of the past as it comes alive in each bite of peanut brittle.

—Jessica B. Harris

PEANUT BRITTLE

2 **cups sugar**
1 **cup light corn syrup**
½ **cup water**
1 **cup (2 sticks) margarine or butter**
2 **cups unsalted or raw peanuts**
1 **teaspoon baking soda**

Mix sugar, syrup and water in heavy 3-quart saucepan. Cook on medium heat until mixture boils and sugar dissolves, stirring constantly with long handled wooden spoon. Stir in margarine until blended.

Stirring frequently, cook until temperature on candy thermometer reaches 280°F or small amount of mixture when dropped into very cold water will stretch into firm but still elastic strands. Stir in peanuts.

Stirring constantly, cook until temperature reaches 305°F or small amount of mixture when dropped in very cold water will solidify and easily snap in half. Remove from heat. Quickly stir in baking soda; mix well. Pour onto 2 nonstick or greased cookie sheets. Spread to edges of pans using back of wooden spoon. Cool slightly. Remove from pans as soon as possible. Break into pieces.

HERITAGE RECIPE

Makes 2½ pounds.

MY MOTHER AURELIA P. NOBLE SAID...

My mother was a very focused, creative and persistent hard worker. I don't ever remember seeing my Mother with idle hands, nor do I remember time demarcations which separated "work time" and "play time"...Like work was to be done from 9 a.m. to 5 p.m. and social activities pursued only on weekends or after work. When there was work to be done or a creative idea to be expressed she gave her all to the tasks at hand. Out in the florist or drapery shop in our backyard she worked and friends and family gathered around, day and night. She made slip covers and draperies and helped my grandparents run a florist shop. Her attitude toward that work was contagious. She could dispense advice while "never missing a stitch!" I think she really never wanted me to work as hard as she did. Today we would call her a "workaholic," and we are taught that's not always the best lifestyle to pursue. But since she loved her work and produced beautiful things, I grew up thinking that working hard to achieve worthwhile goals and things of beauty was not only admirable but enjoyable.

She taught me the value of productive and creative work as one of God's choicest blessings...something to cherish and enjoy.

Years later Alex Haley wrote me about this "work value," possibly inherited from our African ancestors.

"Nightly now, it was on the eve of the annual harvest, circa 1760, every female in the village over twelve rains old, was boiling and then cooling a freshly-pounded saydame solution, in which they soak their feet to a deep, inky blackness up to the ankles; as well as the palms of their hands, as all men felt that the more blackness a woman had, the more beautiful she was — and especially if she was obviously physically strong. So, the Mothers of unmarried daughters were quick to tell them, 'You are beautiful, but you learn to work, for you cannot eat your beauty.'"

Dr. Jeanne L. Noble
Professor
The City University of New York

CELEBRATING OUR MOTHERS' RECIPES FOR KIDS

PASSIN' IT ON

The recipes in this book are the treasured recipes of many of the members of the National Council of Negro Women. These heirlooms are living witnesses to each family's past. They have been passed down and transformed through good times and bad times, through times when food was abundant and times when the stew had to be stretched. These recipes are a part of our communal birthright and our racial heritage; and, as such, they are precious. In writing them down, in many cases for the first time, we are passing them on. This, however, is only the first part of a process. These recipes and the heritage of the African-American dining table must be preserved for future generations, and the only way to do this is to pass them on.

Like a child's game, passing recipes on means taking time out. It is a time that may at first seem to be without quick reward, but the reward is there — not immediately, but in the future. When you take time to teach younger members of a family how to cook a treasured recipe, or when you take daily minutes to re-create that favorite memory which is the family warmth of the dining table, you are not only a caretaker of past traditions, but you are also an investor in the harmony and the hope for the future.

Begin simple: Let smaller children have their kitchen or dining room chores. Let them begin by setting the table, or making sure that the napkins are folded, or being sure that the water glasses are filled. Give them a task. Instruct them in how to do it properly, and make sure that they do it. As they become more involved with the meal, and as they become more used to the kitchen and dining room, they will become more interested in food. This is the first step.

Move on: Teach children about food. Instruct them in the basic food groups and in nutritional values. If you don't know them yourself, or you're not sure, check with your local library or write to the FDA (Food and Drug Administration in Washington, D.C.) for guidelines. As youngsters begin to know more about food and more about healthy eating options, they'll realize all by themselves that fast food may not always be the best food and that there are options for good food within the category of fast food. This is the stage at which you can begin to initiate youngsters into small supervised kitchen activities: washing lettuce and shredding it for salads, arranging and measuring ingredients, and so on. Tasks should be specific and supervised and increased in difficulty as they are mastered. You'll benefit from the extra helping hands in the kitchen, and the youngsters will learn even more about food.

Finally: Begin to allow older children to prepare small meals by themselves, under supervision. Start with something simple, like a bowl of soup and some cheese and crackers or a grilled cheeese sandwich, and then move on to more complicated dishes. Kids' favorites, like some of the recipes in this chapter, can be mastered and will give older children the freedom to prepare healthy foods for themselves if they're home alone or watching younger brothers and sisters.

Don't forget:

Initiate children into the fun of the kitchen early. Be sure to let them in on treasured family recipes. All too often, recipes are forgotten or lost when no one asks about them until it is too late. Let the younger generation watch and participate in the kitchen. Allow them to feel a part of the process and, more importantly, let them know why food is important.

Let them know that it is health, it is survival, and it is history. Pass It On!

—**Jessica B. Harris**

GROUND BEEF & MACARONI

2 **pounds ground beef**
1 **large green pepper, chopped**
1 **medium onion, chopped**
1 **stalk celery, chopped**
1 **package (16 ounces) elbow macaroni, cooked, drained**
1 **package (10 ounces) frozen mixed vegetables, thawed**
1 **package (12 ounces) Kraft deluxe pasteurized process American cheese slices**
3 **eggs**
1 **can (12 ounces) evaporated milk**
½ **teaspoon pepper**

Heat oven to 350°F.

Brown beef with pepper, onion and celery in large skillet on medium heat; drain.

Place ½ of the macaroni in 4-quart shallow casserole. Top with ½ of the beef mixture, vegetables and cheese; repeat layers. Beat eggs in medium bowl; stir in milk and pepper. Pour evenly over casserole; cover loosely with aluminum foil.

Bake 30 to 40 minutes or until hot and bubbly.

Makes 16 servings.

CHILI CASSEROLE

1 **pound ground beef**
1 **package (1¾ ounces) chili seasoning mix**
1 **can (16 ounces) whole kernel corn, drained**
1 **can (16 ounces) red kidney beans, drained**
1 **can (15 ounces) tomato sauce**
1 **cup water**
1 **package (7 ounces) cornbread mix**
1 **egg**
⅓ **cup milk**

Heat oven to 400°F.

Brown beef in large skillet on medium-high heat; drain. Add seasoning mix, corn, beans, tomato sauce and water; bring to boil. Pour into 2½-quart casserole.

Prepare cornbread mix with egg and milk as directed on package. Pour over chili mixture.

Bake 15 to 20 minutes or until cornbread is lightly browned.

Makes 6 servings.

WESTERN SKILLET

1 **pound ground beef**
1 **can (16 ounces) whole peeled tomatoes, cut up**
1¾ **cups water**
1 **package (10 ounces) frozen peas**
1 **envelope (1¼ ounces) onion soup mix**
1 **teaspoon chili powder**
1½ **cups Minute original or premium rice**
1 **cup (4 ounces) shredded Kraft natural cheddar cheese**

Heat oven to 425°F.

Brown meat in large skillet with ovenproof handle (or cover handle with aluminum foil) on medium-high heat. Add tomatoes, water, peas, soup mix and chili powder; bring to boil. Stir in rice; cover. Remove from heat. Let stand 5 minutes. Stir. Sprinkle with cheese.

Bake, uncovered, 10 minutes or until cheese is melted.

Makes 6 servings.

SPAGHETTI SAUCE

1 **pound ground beef**
2 **large onions, chopped**
1 **green pepper, chopped**
1 **clove garlic, minced**
2 **cans (15 ounces each) tomato sauce**
1 **can (28 ounces) crushed tomatoes**
1 **teaspoon seasoning salt**
½ **teaspoon dried oregano leaves**
½ **teaspoon sugar**
¼ **teaspoon pepper Hot cooked spaghetti**

Cook and stir beef, onions, pepper and garlic in large saucepot on medium-high heat until beef is well browned.

Add tomato sauce, tomatoes and seasonings; bring to boil. Reduce heat to low; simmer 20 minutes, stirring occasionally. Serve over spaghetti.

Makes 8 servings.

PIZZA PUFF

2 **cups Stove Top chicken flavor stuffing mix in the canister**
1½ **cups (6 ounces) shredded mozzarella cheese**
1 **can (4 ounces) sliced mushrooms, drained**
2 **ounces sliced pepperoni**
2 **tablespoons flour**
3 **eggs**
2 **cups milk**
1 **teaspoon dried oregano leaves Hot pizza sauce**

Heat oven to 350°F.

Pour stuffing mix into 2-quart baking dish; set aside. Mix cheese, mushrooms, pepperoni and flour in small bowl. Spoon over stuffing mix. Beat eggs in large bowl; stir in milk and oregano. Pour over stuffing mixture.

Bake 30 minutes or until golden brown. Let stand 5 minutes. Serve with heated sauce.

Makes 6 servings.

WEINER SPAGHETTI

5 cups water
1 package
   (8 ounces)
   spaghetti,
   uncooked,
   broken into small
   pieces
1 can (6 ounces)
   tomato paste
6 turkey hot dogs,
   sliced
1 small green
   pepper, chopped
1 small onion,
   chopped
1 stalk celery,
   chopped
1 teaspoon salt
1 teaspoon dried
   oregano leaves
1 tablespoon oil
   Grated Parmesan
   cheese

Bring water to boil in large saucepan. Add all ingredients except cheese; return to boil. Reduce heat to low; simmer, stirring occasionally, 15 minutes or until spaghetti is tender. Serve with grated cheese.

Makes 6 servings.

MY MOTHER GOLDEEN CROFF DICKERSON SAID...

"You will never understand what makes people tick, but if you will remember that there are people who will think exactly the opposite of what you think, and who will do exactly the opposite of what you will do, then it will be a little easier for you to accept the things that happen in life."

Goldeen Dickerson
Elyria, OH

HAMBURGER HURRY UP

2½ **pounds ground beef**
1 **can (16 ounces) pork and beans**
½ **cup firmly packed brown sugar**
1 **cup catsup**

Brown meat in large skillet on medium-high heat; drain. Stir in pork and beans, sugar and catsup. Reduce heat to low; cover and simmer 20 minutes.

Makes 10 servings.

MAC & STUFF

1 **package (14 ounces) Kraft deluxe macaroni & cheese dinner**
1¼ **cups water**
1 **cup frozen green peas**
4 **hot dogs, sliced**
2 **tablespoons Parkay spread stick or butter**
2 **cups Stove Top chicken flavor stuffing mix in the canister**

Prepare dinner as directed on package.

Meanwhile, bring water, peas, hot dogs and spread to boil in large saucepan. Stir in stuffing mix just to moisten; cover. Remove from heat. Let stand 5 minutes.

Gently stir stuffing mixture into prepared dinner. Serve immediately.

Makes 4 servings.

MY MOTHER EMMA MAE OVERSTREET SAID...

"Remember the Golden Rule—you can never go wrong if you do unto others as you would have them do unto you."

**Marian Grace
Cincinnati, OH**

PRESTO-CHANGO SHAKE

3 cups milk
1 envelope
   Kool-Aid bluedini
   flavor
   unsweetened soft
   drink mix*
1 package
   (6-serving size)
   Jell-O vanilla
   flavor instant
   pudding & pie
   filling
1 cup ice cubes

   *Or use any flavor
   Kool-Aid
   unsweetened soft
   drink mix.

Pour milk into blender container. With blender running on lowest speed, add soft drink mix. Add pudding mix; cover and blend until smooth. Add ice cubes; cover and blend on high speed until ice is melted. Serve immediately.

Makes 4 servings.

SUNSHINE FROSTED

3 cups milk*
1 envelope
   Kool-Aid sugar-
   sweetened soft
   drink mix, any
   flavor
1 pint vanilla ice
   cream

Combine milk, soft drink mix and ice cream in blender. Blend for 30 seconds or until smooth. Serve immediately.

Makes 5 servings.

JIGGLERS

2½ cups boiling
    water or boiling
    apple juice (Do
    not add cold
    water.)
2 packages
   (8-serving size) or
   4 packages
   (4-serving size)
   Jell-O brand
   gelatin, any
   flavor

Stir boiling water into gelatin in large bowl 3 minutes or until completely dissolved. Pour into 13x9-inch pan.

Refrigerate at least 3 hours or until firm. Dip bottom of pan in warm water about 15 seconds. Cut into decorative shapes with cookie cutters all the way through gelatin or cut into 1-inch squares.

Makes about 24 pieces.

GIGGLIN' GRAPES

2½ **cups boiling water**
2 **packages (8-serving size) or 4 packages (4-serving size) grape flavor Jell-O brand gelatin**
8 **green gumdrop spearmint leaves**
Assorted candies and fruit
Multi-colored sprinkles
Cool Whip whipped topping
Baker's Angel Flake coconut
Assorted nuts

Stir boiling water into gelatin in medium bowl 2 minutes or until completely dissolved. Pour into 13x9-inch pan. Refrigerate 3 hours or until firm. Cut gelatin into circles, using miniature cookie cutter, round pastry tip or small cap from bottle. Or, cut into cubes.

Arrange gelatin circles on 8 dessert plates, stacking to resemble grape clusters. Use spearmint leaf for stem. Decorate with candies, fruit, sprinkles, whipped topping, coconut and nuts to resemble faces.

Refrigerate until ready to serve.

Makes 8 servings.

CARAMEL CEREAL BARS

20 **caramels**
1 **tablespoon water**
4 **cups Post Golden Crisp cereal**
2 **cups popped popcorn**
½ **cup peanuts (optional)**

Butter 13x9-inch baking pan.

Melt caramels and water in small heavy saucepan on low heat, stirring frequently until smooth. Pour over cereal, popcorn and peanuts in large bowl; mix well. Press firmly into prepared pan.

Refrigerate 1 hour. Cut into bars.

Makes 32.

Microwave preparation: Microwave caramels and water in microwavable bowl on HIGH 2 to 3 minutes or until caramels are melted, stirring every minute. Continue as directed above.

KENTE CLOTH CAKE

Cake:
- 1 package (2-layer size) white cake mix
- 1½ cups boiling water
- 1 package (4-serving size) Jell-O brand gelatin, any flavor
- 1 tub (4 ounces) Cool Whip whipped topping, thawed
- 3 cups Baker's Angel Flake coconut, divided
  Black food coloring paste
  Yellow food coloring paste

Decoration:
  Assorted colorful candies such as orange and red square fruit cherries, grape flavor chewy fruit rolls, green jelly beans, red and black licorice sticks or strings

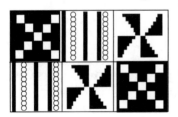

For cake, prepare and bake cake mix as directed on package for 13x9-inch cake. Cool cake 15 minutes; remove from pan. Cool completely on wire rack. Place cake, top side up, in clean 13x9-inch baking pan. Pierce cake with large fork at ½-inch intervals.

Stir boiling water into gelatin in small bowl 2 minutes or until completely dissolved. Carefully pour over cake.

Refrigerate 3 hours. Dip cake pan in warm water 10 seconds; unmold onto serving tray. Frost top and sides of cake with whipped topping.

For decoration, tint 1 cup of the coconut black and 1 cup of the coconut yellow. Reserve 2 tablespoons yellow coconut.

Using long knife, score top of frosted cake into 6 equal squares. Sprinkle 2 squares with black coconut; sprinkle 2 squares with yellow coconut; sprinkle remaining 2 squares with remaining 1 cup untinted coconut. Decorate squares on cake with assorted candies and reserved 2 tablespoons yellow coconut as shown in illustration. Or, use your favorite Kente cloth design and color combinations to create your own Kente pattern. Refrigerate 1 hour or until ready to serve. Store leftover cake in refrigerator.

Makes 12 servings.

BASKETBALL CAKE

Cakes:

- **2 packages (2-layer size each) white cake mix**
- **2 cups boiling water**
- **1 package (8-serving size) or 2 packages (4-serving size) Jell-O brand gelatin, any flavor**
- **1 tub (8 ounces) Cool Whip whipped topping, thawed**

Decoration:

- **4 cups Baker's Angel Flake coconut**
  Red and yellow food coloring
  Black licorice bites, cut to form laces

For cakes, prepare and bake first cake mix as directed on package for 12-cup fluted tube pan. Cool 15 minutes; remove from pans. Cool completely on wire rack. Repeat with second cake mix. Place cakes in clean 12-cup fluted tube pans. Pierce cakes with large fork at ½-inch intervals.

Stir boiling water into gelatin in large bowl 2 minutes or until completely dissolved. Carefully pour ½ of the gelatin over each cake.

Refrigerate 3 hours. Dip 1 cake pan in warm water 10 seconds; unmold rounded side down onto serving plate. Spread flat top surface with small amount whipped topping. Unmold second cake; carefully place on top of first cake, pressing flat sides together. Frost top and sides of cake with remaining whipped topping.

For decoration, tint coconut orange using red and yellow food colorings. Sprinkle over cake. Decorate with black licorice to look like a basket ball. Refrigerate 1 hour or until ready to serve. Store leftover cake in refrigerator.

Makes 24 servings.

MY MOTHER GLORIA B. CAPONIS SAID...

*M*y Mother was a great cook. Among her many specialties was one of my favorites, seafood gumbo. I spent most of my life learning how to make Momie's special seafood gumbo. She used shrimp and crabs as her base. In the South, crabs were "dressed crabs." We always bought them like that at home. ("Dressed crabs," for those who are not from the South, are crabs that have been cleaned and are ready to "drop" in the pot).

One New Year's Eve, My Momie was visiting me and it took a lot of doing to convince her to make her seafood gumbo. It was 6 p.m. on New Year's Eve when she finally agreed to make it if I could get her "dressed crabs." I happily invited about 20 people to join us to welcome in the New Year.

We went to the wharf to get the seafood. Momie went over to a boat that had crabs on display and asked for "a dozen dressed crabs, please." The man looked at her. Then he looked at me. Then he looked back at her and said, "Ma'm, we don't put clothes on our crabs."

We bought the crabs and took them home to "dress" them for the gumbo. Momie's seafood gumbo was ready for our guests at exactly 12:01 a.m. of the New Year.

The moral of the story is — do not ask for "dressed crabs" except in the South and never, never ask your mother to make her special seafood gumbo with only four hours to prepare it.

Alexis M. Herman
Assistant to the President and Director of Public Liaison
The White House,
Washington, DC

CELEBRATING OUR MOTHERS' PRESERVES

PUTTIN' IT UP

Ever since the first man presented his cave wife with a freshly slaughtered bison, the question of how to preserve an overabundance of food for leaner times has been uppermost in the minds of most homemakers. This is true, too, in the African-American world when all-too-frequent hard times made preserving and conserving bumper crops of fruits and vegetables, meats and grains a necessity. Today, in our era of massive deep freezers and supermarkets brimming with peaches, watermelons and cherries in December, it's difficult to imagine that, up until relatively recent times, the only way that fresh vegetables were available in the winter months was if they had been "put up" by an industrious cook.

While the necessity of "putting up" foods for the winter no longer remains, it is undeniable that nothing can quite beat the taste of foods captured at the peak of their ripeness and freshness by a home cook. Eva Woods Webster of Florence, Alabama is one such enterprising cook who delights in her canning and her putting up and whose annual calendar follows that of the seasons in much the same way that our foremothers' did.

She recalls, "I come from a long line of food-smart people. My granddaddy would farm. You name it and he had it growing somewhere. We were a big family. There were nine children. Things were kind of tough and we had to preserve foods as best we could. We dried things and canned things for winter. We farmed and raised potatoes and stored them in mounds we called 'hillum.' We also grew turnips and kept them the same way. Other items involved more preparation.

"I started cooking when I was eight years old. I was the second child as we came along, and every girl would take her share. I began working with the canning when I was around ten or eleven. I was always the kind of child who was always watching adults, and one day I just began to help with stringing beans. We'd snap 'em, string 'em, blanch 'em, and put them in their jars with the solution. That's how I came about learning...from doing. I always wanted to learn. At age thirteen, I began to do domestic work for other people, and I learned a lot from that too.

"At home, we had a canning schedule. You'd start canning when things are ripe and ready. Green cabbage and peas start around the end of May. The cabbage begins to head in late April, and by May and June, we would make kraut. Then came the green beans and beets and potatoes. Then came field peas and crowder peas and corn. I still can some of them today, but I also freeze a lot of it. I freeze my corn and I freeze what we call English peas or green peas. I still can some okra, too. It's easy. You cut off the back part of the stem high enough to keep the 'slaver' from running out of it and then blanch it.

"Cucumbers are fairly early around here, and when they're ready, we make pickles or relish. There are one-day pickles, fourteen-day pickles, bread and butter pickles, and more. I started out with recipes, and then I got so I just began to experiment with things. You get so you know and you get it down pat. I also make chow chow, which starts with cabbage.

"My favorite canned goods are my pear preserves, my bread and butter pickles, and my blackberry jelly. I used to live where I could go out and just pick 'goo-goos' of blackberries, but now I have to buy my berries. I guess that's progress.

"Everyone doesn't have time for canning nowadays. I think that if you think you don't have time, but you'd still like to try, you should plan to can and preserve at night or in the evening. You have to have a lot of motivation and a lot of push. It takes a lot of time and energy, but it's worth it. I guess it's my hobby; I love to cook. I guess my home is the house beside the road. I always have someone dropping by, and I just love to cook. It's just a part of my life."

-Jessica B. Harris

SECRETS OF SUCCESS

How to make delicious jams and jellies:

BEFORE YOU START

- Read recipe before beginning. Follow directions EXACTLY!
- **Do not** substitute brands of fruit pectin in recipes. Each brand of fruit pectin has a different formulation.
- **Do not** double recipes as the mixture may not set. When a recipe is doubled, there is not enough surface area in the saucepot nor adequate boiling time for a sufficient amount of liquid to evaporate.
- Assemble your equipment and measure ingredients before starting.
- Make sure your jars are spotless and free of cracks or nicks.
- Use a 6- or 8-quart flat-bottomed saucepot that is made of stainless steel, enameled metal or a hard-coat aluminum pan that will not change the color or flavor of the fruit or vegetable. It is important to use the size of pot specified as the surface area of the pot determines how much liquid will evaporate.

PREPARING THE FRUIT

- Use ripe fruits (not under- or overripe) that are thoroughly rinsed with clear water. Drain.
- For berries, crush 1 cup at a time, using a potato masher for best results. If using a food processor, pulse to chop the fruit. **Do not**

puree. Jam should contain pieces of fruit.
- You can use unsweetened frozen fruit. Thaw fruit to room temperature before crushing to equal the same amount of crushed fresh fruit. **Do not** drain off excess juice.
- To prevent browning of light-colored fruits in jams and jellies, add 1 teaspoon of lemon juice to prepared fruit.

PREPARING THE JARS

- **NEW! The makers of CERTO® have found a way to eliminate the step of boiling jars in preparation for making jams and jellies. Because of the high sugar and acid contents of jams and jellies, jar preparation can be handled by the Inversion Method described on page 199. *IMPORTANT! This method applies only to jam and jelly recipes.* When preserving all other foods, follow recommended USDA water bath or pressure canning methods.**
- Use new, flat lids every time. They cannot be reused.
- Wash jars, lids and bands thoroughly before you begin so they will be ready when the jam or jelly is ready to pour. Place flat lids in a saucepan. Pour boiling water over the lids. Let stand in hot water until ready to fill jars. (The hot water softens the rubber and helps create a seal.) Drain jars and lids well before filling.

MAKING JAMS AND JELLIES

- **DO NOT REDUCE SUGAR OR USE SUGAR SUBSTITUTES**. The exact amounts of sugar, fruit and pectin are necessary for a good set.
- Use a **liquid** (glass or plastic) measuring cup with a pour spout to measure fruit. Use a **dry** (metal or plastic) measuring cup with a straight top edge to measure sugar. (Tip: A 5-pound bag of sugar equals about 12 cups.)
- Use regular granulated sugar, **NOT** EXTRA FINE. Do not use sugar blends with dextrose, fructose or other sweeteners added. The recipes in this book were tested with granulated cane sugar.
- **Do not** eliminate lemon juice if a recipe calls for it. For jelling to occur, there must be a precise balance of sugar, fruit, pectin and acid.
- It is essential to get a full rolling boil for jam or jelly to set. **Boil for amount of time specified**. A full rolling boil is a boil that does not stop when stirred.
- Add margarine or butter to keep foaming to a minimum.
- When making jelly, moisten the jelly bag or cheesecloth first, wring it out, and then pour the fruit into it. A dry bag can absorb a lot of juice. For clear jelly, **do not** squeeze the bag. Fruit pulp gets into juice.
- Keep fruit juice in an airtight container and freeze it up to 6 months for later use.
- For clear jelly, ladle jelly **quickly** into jars. This eliminates trapped air bubbles which can make jelly look cloudy.

FILLING THE JARS

- Prepare jam or jelly recipe as directed.
- Fill all jam and jelly jars immediately to within ⅛ inch of tops.
- Wipe jars' rims and threads with a clean, damp cloth. Cover quickly with flat lids. Screw bands on tightly. Invert jars 5 minutes, then turn upright.
- Paraffin seals are not recommended for jams and jellies, particularly in warm and humid climates where molds grow readily.

THE PROPER SEAL

In most areas of the country, the inversion method for sealing jars protects adequately against mold. Contaminants which may cause spoilage are destroyed when hot fruit mixtures are immediately poured, covered and inverted for 5 minutes to seal after the jam or jelly is cooked. In very warm or humid climates, however, sealing jars by the USDA water bath method can provide additional protection.

Inversion method: Immediately after pouring hot fruit mixture into jars, cover and invert jars on their tops for 5 minutes. Turn upright. After jars cool, check seals. See below.

Water Bath Method (Recommended by the USDA): Place jars on a rack in a canner or large saucepot of boiling water. The water should cover the jars by 1 to 2 inches. Cover the canner and bring water to a boil; boil 5 minutes for 8-ounce jars; boil 10 minutes for 16-ounce jars. Remove the jars from the canner. Let jars stand to cool. Check seals.

Sealed Jars: Lids should be concave (curve down) and stay that way when pressed lightly. If the jar is not sealed (the lid pops up when pressed), either re-process by removing jar contents and filling and sealing again **or** let jams and jellies set for 24 hours and refrigerate and use within three weeks.

STORING JARS

- Wipe jars of cooled jams and jellies with a clean, damp cloth before storing. Label jars with flavors and dates. Store unopened jars in a cool, dry, dark place.
- Use unopened cooked jams and jellies within 1 year of making. Once opened, store in refrigerator and use within 3 weeks.
- If a jam or jelly has mold on it, discard the entire jar.

Jam and Jelly making guidelines courtesy of Kraft General Foods, Inc.

PEAR JAM

4 cups prepared fruit (about 3 pounds fully ripe Bartlett pears)
7½ cups sugar
¼ cup lemon juice
½ teaspoon margarine or butter
1 pouch Certo liquid fruit pectin

Peel and core pears; finely chop. Measure 4 cups fruit into 6 or 8-quart saucepot. Stir in sugar and lemon juice; set aside for 10 minutes, stirring occasionally.

Prepare jars (see directions on page 198). Keep lids hot until ready to fill jars.

Stir fruit mixture in saucepot. Add margarine. Bring mixture to full rolling boil (one that does not stop when stirred) on high heat, stirring constantly. Quickly stir in fruit pectin. Return to full rolling boil and boil exactly 1 minute, stirring constantly. Remove from heat. Skim off any foam with metal spoon.

Ladle quickly into prepared jars, filling to within ⅛ inch of tops. Wipe jar rims and threads. Cover quickly with flat lids. Screw bands tightly. Invert jars 5 minutes, then turn upright. After jars are cool, check seals.

Makes 8 (1 cup) jars.

MY MOTHER EMMA J. "MOMMY" HANCOCK SAID...

"Hold your head up high and don't be afraid to take a chance in life."

Georgia A. Overton
Inwood Long Island, NY

GRAPE JELLY

4 **cups prepared juice (about 3 pounds fully ripe grapes and ½ cup water)**
7 **cups sugar**
½ **teaspoon margarine or butter**
1 **pouch Certo liquid fruit pectin**

Remove stems and slip skins from grapes. Crush, one layer at a time. Place grape pulp in saucepan; add ½ cup water. Bring to boil. Reduce heat; cover and simmer 10 minutes. Place in jelly cloth or bag and let drip. When dripping has almost ceased, press gently. Measure 4 cups into 6 or 8-quart saucepot.

Prepare jars (see directions on page 198). Keep lids hot until ready to fill jars.

Mix sugar thoroughly into fruit juice in saucepot. Add margarine. Bring mixture to full rolling boil (one that does not stop when stirred) on high heat, stirring constantly. Quickly stir in fruit pectin. Return to full rolling boil and boil exactly 1 minute, stirring constantly. Remove from heat. Skim off any foam with metal spoon.

Ladle quickly into prepared jars, filling to within ⅛ inch of tops. Wipe jar rims and threads. Cover quickly with flat lids. Screw bands tightly. Invert jars 5 minutes, then turn upright. After jars are cool, check seals.

Makes 6 (1 cup) jars.

MY MOTHER ALMETTA HERICE JOHNS SAID...

"No matter what, pay your rent so that whatever happens, you will always have a roof over your head."

Dorothy Joyce Johns
San Francisco, CA

TOMATO RELISH

3 **cups prepared tomatoes (about 2¼ pounds fully ripe tomatoes)***
1½ **teaspoons grated lemon peel**
¼ **cup lemon juice**
6½ **cups sugar**
½ **teaspoon margarine or butter**
2 **pouches Certo liquid fruit pectin**

Or use 2½ pounds fully ripe yellow tomatoes and ½ cup lemon juice.

Scald, peel and chop tomatoes. Place in 4-quart saucepan. Bring to boil; reduce heat, cover and simmer 10 minutes. Measure 3 cups into 6 or 8-quart saucepot. Add lemon peel and juice.

Prepare jars (see directions on page 198). Keep lids hot until ready to fill jars.

Mix sugar thoroughly into tomatoes in saucepot. Add margarine. Bring mixture to full rolling boil (one that does not stop when stirred) on high heat, stirring constantly. Quickly stir in fruit pectin. Return to full rolling boil and boil exactly 1 minute, stirring constantly. Remove from heat. Skim off any foam with metal spoon.

Ladle quickly into prepared jars, filling to within ⅛ inch of tops. Wipe jar rims and threads. Cover quickly with flat lids. Screw bands tightly. Invert jars 5 minutes, then turn upright. After jars are cool, check seals.

Makes 7 (1 cup) jars.

MY MOTHER FLORA GRAY SAID...
"Experience is the best teacher."

Mary Haywood-Benson
Champaign, IL

LOTSA PEPPERS RELISH

3 **cups prepared peppers (2 medium red peppers, 2 medium green peppers and 10 large jalapeño peppers)**
1 **cup cider vinegar**
5¼ **cups sugar**
½ **teaspoon margarine or butter**
1 **pouch Certo liquid fruit pectin**

Stem and halve all peppers; discard seeds. Finely chop or grind peppers. Measure 3 cups into 6 or 8-quart saucepot. Stir in vinegar.

Prepare jars (see directions on page 198). Keep lids hot until ready to fill jars.

Mix sugar thoroughly into peppers in saucepot. Add margarine. Bring mixture to full rolling boil (one that does not stop when stirred) on high heat, stirring constantly. Quickly stir in fruit pectin. Return to full rolling boil and boil exactly 1 minute, stirring constantly. Remove from heat. Skim off any foam with metal spoon.

Ladle quickly into prepared jars, filling to within ⅛ inch of tops. Wipe jar rims and threads. Cover quickly with flat lids. Screw bands tightly. Invert jars 5 minutes, then turn upright. After jars are cool, check seals.

Makes 6 (1 cup) jars.

MY MOTHER HENRY LEE "DUCK" HOUCH SAID...

"Keep God first and everything else will follow."

**Yvonne Houch
Bronx, NY**

STRAWBERRY-RHUBARB JAM

4 cups prepared
    fruit (about
    1 quart fully ripe
    strawberries,
    1 pound fully ripe
    rhubarb and
    ½ cup water)
6½ cups sugar
½ teaspoon
    margarine or
    butter
1 pouch Certo
    liquid fruit pectin

Stem and thoroughly crush strawberries, 1 cup at a time. Measure 2¼ cups into 6 or 8-quart saucepot. Finely chop rhubarb; do not peel. Place in 2-quart saucepan. Add ½ cup water. Bring to boil. Reduce heat; cover and simmer 2 minutes or until rhubarb is soft. Measure 1¾ cups into saucepot.

Prepare jars (see directions on page 198). Keep lids hot until ready to fill jars.

Mix sugar thoroughly into fruit in saucepot. Add margarine. Bring mixture to full rolling boil (one that does not stop when stirred) on high heat, stirring constantly. Quickly stir in fruit pectin. Return to full rolling boil and boil exactly 1 minute, stirring constantly. Remove from heat. Skim off any foam with metal spoon.

Ladle quickly into prepared jars, filling to within ⅛ inch of tops. Wipe jar rims and threads. Cover quickly with flat lids. Screw bands tightly. Invert jars 5 minutes, then turn upright. After jars are cool, check seals.

Makes 7 (1 cup) jars.

MY MOTHER MILDRED T. "MAZEY" MAZE SAID...

"Know that everything you do—right or wrong—there are other people who will be affected by your actions."

Wanda C. Maze
Cleveland, OH

PEACH JAM

4 **cups prepared fruit (about 3 pounds fully ripe peaches)**
¼ **cup lemon juice**
7½ **cups sugar**
½ **teaspoon margarine or butter**
1 **pouch Certo liquid fruit pectin**

Peel, pit and finely chop peaches. Measure 4 cups fruit into 6 or 8-quart saucepot. Add lemon juice.

Prepare jars (see directions on page 198). Keep lids hot until ready to fill jars.

Mix sugar thoroughly into fruit in saucepot. Add margarine. Bring mixture to full rolling boil (one that does not stop when stirred) on high heat, stirring constantly. Quickly stir in fruit pectin. Return to full rolling boil and boil exactly 1 minute, stirring constantly. Remove from heat. Skim off any foam with metal spoon.

Ladle quickly into prepared jars, filling to within ⅛ inch of tops. Wipe jar rims and threads. Cover quickly with flat lids. Screw bands tightly. Invert jars 5 minutes, then turn upright. After jars are cool, check seals.

Makes 8 (1 cup) jars.

MY MOTHER GEORGIA LEE SIMONS SAID...

"Apple pie without cheese is like a kiss without a squeeze." I always make sure we have cheese with apple pie.

Shirley J. Wells
Staten Island, NY

APPLE BUTTER

4 cups prepared fruit (about 3 pounds fully ripe tart apples*, 3 cups water and ¼ cup lemon juice)
3 cups sugar
2⅓ cups (1 pound) firmly packed light brown sugar
½ teaspoon margarine or butter
1 pouch Certo liquid fruit pectin

*McIntosh, Cortland, Empire, Beacon or Granny Smith

Remove blossom and stem ends from apples; do not peel or core. Quarter apples. Place in 4-quart saucepan; add 3 cups water and ¼ cup lemon juice. Bring to boil. Reduce heat; cover and simmer 15 minutes. Strain mixture through coarse sieve, using wooden spoon to force apples through sieve; discard peels and seeds. Return apple mixture to 4-quart saucepan. Bring to boil. Reduce heat to medium; cook, uncovered, 30 minutes, stirring occasionally. Measure 4 cups into 6 or 8-quart saucepot.

Prepare jars (see directions on page 198). Keep lids hot until ready to fill jars.

Mix sugars thoroughly into fruit in saucepot. Add margarine. Bring mixture to full rolling boil (one that does not stop when stirred) on high heat, stirring constantly. Quickly stir in fruit pectin. Return to full rolling boil and boil exactly 1 minute, stirring constantly. Remove from heat. Skim off any foam with metal spoon.

Ladle quickly into prepared jars, filling to within ⅛ inch of tops. Wipe jar rims and threads. Cover quickly with flat lids. Screw bands tightly. Invert jars 5 minutes, then turn upright. After jars are cool, check seals.

Makes 7 (1 cup) jars.

MY MOTHER MARIAN GRACE SAID...

"Always seek positive people to build friendships with."

Anita Grace
Cincinnati, OH

HOW TO MAKE DELICIOUS PICKLED FRUITS & VEGETABLES

BEFORE YOU START

- Read recipe completely before beginning. Follow directions **EXACTLY**!
- Assemble your equipment and measure ingredients before starting.
- Make sure your jars are spotless and free of cracks or nicks.
- Use a 6- or 8-quart flat-bottomed saucepot that is made of stainless steel, enameled metal or a hard-coat aluminum pan that will not change the color or flavor of the fruit or vegetable.

PREPARING THE PRODUCE

- Use ripe produce (not under- or overripe) that is thoroughly rinsed with clear water. Drain.

PREPARING THE JARS

- Use new, flat jar lids every time. They cannot be reused.
- Wash jars, lids and bands thoroughly before you begin so they will be ready when the pickle products are ready to pack. Pour hot (180°F) water over the lids. Let stand in hot water until ready to fill jars. (The hot water softens the rubber and helps create a seal.) Drain jars and lids well before filling.

PACKING PICKLED PRODUCTS

- Remove pickle products from pickling solution and pack into jars according to directions in recipe. Use just enough for one canner load at a time.
- Fill jars immediately with hot fruit or vegetables and pickling solution to within ¼ inch of tops.
- Remove air bubbles from jars by running a non-metallic spatula between the contents and the jar.
- Wipe jars' rims and threads with a clean, damp cloth. Cover quickly with flat lids. Screw bands down evenly and firmly.

PROPER PROCESSING

The water bath method is recommended by the USDA.
- Place each jar as it is filled on rack in a canner or large saucepot of boiling water. The water should cover the jars by 1 to 2 inches. Cover canner and bring water to boil. Adjust heat to hold water at a steady

boil. Start counting processing time when water reaches a full boil. If, during processing time, water should boil away and the tops of jars become exposed, add **boiling** water to cover by 1 to 2 inches. Water should maintain a full boil through the entire processing period.

- When processing time is completed, remove the jars from the canner. Let jars stand to cool, out of drafts and with space between them.
- After 12 to 24 hours, remove bands and test seals. Lids should be concave (curve down) and stay that way when pressed lightly in the center. If a lid fails to seal on a jar, remove the lid and check the jar-sealing surface for tiny nicks. If necessary, change the jar. Heat the product, jar and new lids and repack as before.

STORING JARS

- Wipe jars of cooled pickle products with a clean, damp cloth before storing. Label jars with product name and date. Store unopened jars in a cool, dry, dark place.
- Use unopened pickled products within 1 year of making. Once opened, store in refrigerator.

Pickling guidelines were made available courtesy of the Consumer Affairs Department of Alltrista Corporation and are consistent with USDA recommendations.

MY MOTHER DORIS HARGROVE SAID...

"Always have money for a telephone call."

Scherwin Hargrove
Fairfax, VA

GREEN TOMATO RELISH

2½ **quarts green tomatoes, chopped (7 cups)**
1 **large onion, chopped (1 cup)**
2 **large green peppers, chopped (2 cups)**
6 **small red or green hot peppers, seeded & chopped* (½ cup)**
¼ **cup salt**
2¼ **cups vinegar**
¾ **cup sugar**
½ **cup firmly packed brown sugar**
2 **tablespoons mustard seed**
1½ **teaspoons turmeric**

*When cutting or seeding hot peppers, wear rubber gloves to prevent hands from burning. Avoid contact with eyes.

Combine vegetables in large bowl; sprinkle with salt and mix thoroughly. Let stand 3 hours; drain. Press to remove extra liquid; drain.

Combine vinegar, sugars and spices in 6 or 8-quart saucepot. Bring to boil. Reduce heat; cover and simmer 15 minutes. Add vegetables; return to boil.

Pack mixture into prepared jars, to within ¼ inch of tops. Remove air bubbles. Cover with flat lids. Screw bands down evenly and firmly. Process 10 minutes in boiling water bath (according to directions on page 207).

Makes 6 (1 pint) jars.

MY MOTHER JULIA "JJ" OR "GRAN GRAN" JOHNSON SAID...

"Always wear a smile....People will treat you better when you greet them."
Beverly L. Johnson
Silver Spring, MD

WATERMELON RIND PICKLE

2 tablespoons salt
1 quart cold water, divided
3 cups watermelon rind, cut into 1-inch pieces
2 cups sugar
1½ cups vinegar
1½ cups water
1 tablespoon pickling spices

Dissolve salt in 2 cups of the water; pour over rind in large bowl. Let stand 5 hours. Drain; rinse and drain again. Cover with remaining 2 cups water; let stand 30 minutes. Drain.

Place rind in large saucepan; add enough water to cover. Bring to a boil. Reduce heat; cover and simmer 10 minutes or until fork tender. Drain and set aside.

Combine sugar, vinegar and 1½ cups water in 6 or 8-quart saucepot. Place pickling spices in cheesecloth bag; add to saucepot. Bring to boil. Reduce heat; cover and simmer 5 minutes. Add rind; bring to boil. Reduce heat; cover and simmer 20 minutes or until syrup thickens. Remove spice bag.

Pack mixture into prepared jars, to within ¼ inch of tops. Remove air bubbles. Cover with flat lids. Screw bands down evenly and firmly. Process 20 minutes in boiling water bath (according to directions on page 207).

Makes 3 (1 cup) jars.

MY MOTHER HELEN B. "RED" SMITH SAID...

"Never look down on anyone no matter how high you climb."

**Myrtle E. Marshall
Cincinnati, OH**

CHOW CHOW PICKLES

2½ **quarts green tomatoes, chopped (7 cups)**
2 **large onions, chopped (2 cups)**
1 **medium head cabbage, chopped (5 cups)**
3 **tablespoons salt**
2½ **cups vinegar**
2 **cups sugar**
1 **tablespoon pickling spices**
1 **teaspoon pepper**

Combine vegetables in large bowl; sprinkle with salt and mix thoroughly. Let stand 4 hours; drain.

Combine vinegar and sugar in 6 or 8-quart saucepot. Place pickling spices in cheesecloth bag; add to saucepot with pepper. Bring to boil. Reduce heat; cover and simmer 10 minutes. Add vegetables; return to boil. Reduce heat; cover and simmer 10 minutes. Remove spice bag.

Pack mixture into prepared jars, to within ¼ inch of tops. Remove air bubbles. Cover with flat lids. Screw bands down evenly and firmly. Process 10 minutes in boiling water bath (according to directions on page 207).

Makes 11 (1 cup) jars.

MY MOTHER ELLA STEPLIGHT SAID...

"Get all the knowledge you can. What goes in your head no one can take away."

Coriner Johnson
East Orange, NJ

HOT SLAW

Salad:
- 12 **cups shredded cabbage (about 2 pounds)**
- 2 **large green peppers, thinly sliced**
- 4 **large carrots, shredded**
- ¾ **cup chopped onion**
- 1 **tablespoon salt**

Dressing:
- 2 **cups prepared mustard**
- 2 **cups sugar**
- ¾ **cup vinegar**
- ¼ **cup water**
- 1 **tablespoon salt**
- 1 **tablespoon pepper**
- 1 **teaspoon crushed red pepper**

For salad, toss cabbage, peppers, carrots and onion in large bowl. Sprinkle with salt. Let stand 1 hour; drain.

For dressing, stir mustard, sugar, vinegar, water, salt and peppers in large saucepan. Bring to boil. Boil 3 minutes. Cool. Pour over cabbage mixture; let stand 5 minutes. Stir well. Spoon into clean plastic containers to within ½ inch of top. Wipe off top edges of containers; cover with lids. Freeze.

Makes 20 cups.

PICKLED OKRA

- 2 **pounds small okra pods, washed and cleaned**
- 12 **cloves garlic**
- 6 **small red or green hot peppers**
- 2 **cups water**
- 2 **cups vinegar**
- 2 **tablespoons salt**
- 1 **tablespoon dill seed**

Pack okra, 2 cloves garlic and 1 whole pepper tightly into each prepared jar, to within ¼ inch of tops.

Combine water, vinegar, salt and dill seed in large saucepan. Bring to boil; pour hot liquid slowly over vegetables in jars to within ¼ inch of tops. Remove air bubbles. Cover with flat lids. Screw bands down evenly and firmly. Process 15 minutes in boiling water bath (according to directions on page 207).

Makes 6 (1 pint) jars.

EPILOGUE

When I was in high school, I won a college scholarship in an Elks oratorical contest on the Constitution of the United States. I will never forget my Mother saying to me proudly, "Well, it really sounded better in the auditorium than in the kitchen." While preparing the dinner, my Mother had followed my speech as I practiced it.

In so many ways, the values and ideas that were given in the kitchen or at the dinner table come back to me almost every day. Even her demand that I clean up before coming to the table, which I resisted at the time, has stood me well.

At the National Council of Negro Women, we have learned that values are taught and carried in many simple ways. So it was that in 1986 we began the Black Family Reunion Celebrations. Millions across the country have come together to celebrate our historic African-American strengths and our valued traditions. The food, the entertainment, the educational and recreational activities all have brought renewed appreciation of family life and created a sense of what can happen as the community becomes more like the extended family. And given the need for preserving our history of accomplishment against the odds and of providing motivation to meet the challenges of the future, we have embarked on the creation of the National Center for African-American Women in the nation's capital.

I hope you find in the memories shared in this book something of value and substance as you move through the days ahead. Our lives are enriched with remembrances of our principal caregiver, whether Mother or Father, Grandparent, Aunt or extended family member. They make us mindful of so many simple and inexpensive ways to provide a nurturing environment for each other. How often do we revere a past in which whether we had little or much, we had a sense of the warmth and strength symbolized by our Mothers' kitchens.

Dr. Dorothy I. Height
President/CEO
National Council of Negro Women, Inc.

THE NATIONAL CENTER FOR AFRICAN-AMERICAN WOMEN

The founder of the National Council of Negro Women (NCNW), Mary McLeod Bethune, had a vision of giving African-American women national voice and community responsiveness for social and economic justice. Her vision is even more timely in meeting the increasingly complex and challenging issues of today's world.

The NCNW, under the leadership of Dorothy I. Height, has envisioned the establishment of the National Center for African-American Women in Washington, D.C. to provide the primary resource and the crucial link to leadership, programs, ideas, resources and education on all aspects affecting quality of life for African-American women well into the next century.

Working under the NCNW umbrella, affiliated organizations will spearhead the drive to put into action the mission so relevant today: to recognize and meet the crucial needs of African-American women and their families in the communities where they live and to represent African-American women as an agent for positive change working with public and private sector leadership.

A vast clearinghouse of resources and know-how specific to addressing the issues African-American women and their families face will be immediately accessible to communities via the Center's emerging database and advanced communications capability.

The Center will provide an environment to bring issues of the greatest importance to the national forefront. Ongoing activities at the Center will underscore the valuable contributions African-American women make to fabric of American life. But most importantly, the Center will educate and keep leadership informed on the concepts, policies and strategies for effecting positive change on behalf of African-American women and their families. The Center will also provide a meaningful venue for the release of important findings, reports and academic papers. Ongoing exhibits and seminars open to the public will make the Center an important cultural destination for visitors and residents of Washington, D.C.

The Center will also house the national headquarters of the NCNW, which will work vigorously in the Bethune spirit and tradition "to leave no one behind."

Evelyn Rose Pigford Acree
Starlee Alexander
Evelyn L. Allen
Allene W. Alix
LaTanga Iris Allen
Mary E. Allen
Shirley A. Allen
Martha P. Alston
Sabel-Wengel Ambaye
Naomi C. Andrews
Ain Ashby
Velma Bagley
Marjorie D. Ball
Catherine J. Barbour
Juanita Maria Barnes
Louise Trigg Barnes
Shawn Barrick
Josie M. Barrow
Dorothy R. Bates
Nichole Belk
Belva M. Bell
Marian F. Bell
Tracy Massey Bell
Linda Bellack
Sarah Benjamin
Carolyn Wade Blackett
Helen P. Blocker
Florence Beth Bonner
Zephorah Booker
Marvin R. Boone
Barbara Briley Bond
O. LaVelle Bond
Lillie Bowles
Carol Boyd
Ruby Bright
Dolores L. "Dee" Brinkley
Howard Britt
Ruth B. Britton
Emma B. Broman
Catherine "Kitty" McElroy
    Brooks
Annie Bell Brooks
Earamichia N. Brown
Gladys B. Brown
Jay-Me Brown
Jewlene Wade Brown
John T. Brown
June H. Brown
Doris Brown-Billingsley
Carneice Brown-White
Mary Burciaga
Yvonne D. Burkhalter
Felicia Burress
Diane Butler
Shirley Butler
Virginia Byrd
Bernice Caffey
Bettye Washington
    Campbell

Maria V. Carobello
Kitty Chaney
Richard John Champion
Jarnice Chapman
Gloria L. Chapmon
Celestine W. Cheek
Auther Mae Chewe
Vera Lee Clanton
Christy F. Clark
Magetta Clue
Dr. Johnnetta B. Cole
Carlotte Coleman
James C. Comer
Brenda Rhodes Cooper
Camille Cosby
Debbie Short Craddock
Shereen M. Craig
Val Creighton
Veronica Cumberland
Sharon K. Curry
Brenda Dalton-James
John T. Daniel, Jr.
Ida Daniel Dark
Beatrice E. "Lacy" Davis
Goldeen Dickerson
Zelda Dixon-LeCoat
Angeline Gallman
    Donaldson
Julie Donaldson
Al Douglas, Jr.
Brenda Dunnigan
Dorothy Durden-
    Thompson
Gracie Echols
Ramona H. Edelin
Bessie R. Edwards
Ruby Edwards
Roselyn Payne Epps
Theresa Essel
Eva. L. Evans
Evelyn S. Field
Dawna Michelle Fields
Betty Ford
Dora Bell Fortune
Jylla Moore Foster
Mr. R. L. Fowler
Mr. V. P. Fowler
Mrs. A. Fowler
Sandra R. Fowler
Bernice Franklin
Martha Frazier
Jacqueline Frazier-Stewart
Lillie Freeman
Ardenia Gamble
Bettye J. Gardner
Maggie Jean Gardner
Dora L. Garner
Alice J. McCullough Garrett
Carol Thomas Garretson

Beulah Ross Gaskin
Earline Gates
Lucille Jordan Gayle
Dorothy Gerald
Rachel M. Gibson
Deidre Kym Gibson
Patricia Gibson
Judy Gilchriest
Frankie Jacobs Gillette
Brenda M. Girton
Vern Goff
Queen E. M. Gordon
Anita Grace
Marian Grace
Mattie Grant
Jo Anne Stovall Gray
Patricia Grayson
Ellen Grayson-Barnes
Joan Green
Carolyn Hailey Grey
Dorothy Grier
Alice T. Griffin
Alzeda C. Hacker
Nettie D. Hailes
Cathy Cobb Halford
Mary Catherine Hamilton
Sara S. Hampton
Deborah Harden
William Harding
Corlista H. Hardman
Rochelle Hardy
Queen. E. Hargett
Scherwin Hargrove
Mary L. Harris
Cheryl Harris-Lee
Wilma Harvey
Brin D. Hawkins
Mary Haywood-Benson
Marlene A. Harris
Mattie L. Haywood
Dorothy I. Height
Alexis M. Herman
Linda O. Herring
Gloria Thomas Hicks
Willa Mae Hicks
Marjorie Hill-Fields
Rubye B. Hill
Elizabeth Hines
Vivian E. Hoban
Dorethea Nelson
    Hornbuckle
Lucille A. Horton
Yvonne Houch
Vivian E. Howard
Edna Huggins
Esther Huggins
Catherine Liggins Hughes
Dawn Hughes
Jacqueline Hughes

Stella Fleming Hughes
Cassandra Hughes-Webster
Lee Dorothy Humes
Bettye S. Hunt
Lillie Hunter
Charlayne Hunter-Gault
Economy F. Jackson
Kayla Jackson
Gwen Jarvis
Issie L. Shelton Jenkins
Dorothy Joyce Johns
Angela W. Johnson
Beverly L. Johnson
Coriner Johnson
Helena Johnson
L. Patricia Johnson
Lillie B. F. Johnson
Thelma H. Johnson
Theresa M. Johnson
Christin B. Jones
Diana N. Jones
Mary Jones-Hills
Willie B. Kennedy
Katherine Kennedy
Virgil Mae Kenney
Coretta Scott King
Pamela Kirkland
Patti LaBelle
Janet C. Lane
Velma T. Lassister
Unita L. Lawrence
Clara Sturdivant Lee
Corrine Lee
Mary E. Leftenant
Audrey V. Lennon
Sarah C. Leonard
Doris B. Lockhart
Melissa M. Luck
Marjorie Robinson
    MacKerrow
L. Dianne Webster Madyun
Julianne Malveaux
Myrtle E. Marshall
Codis F. Martin
Rabihah A. Mateen
Barbara Watts Maxwell
Wanda C. Maze
Bernice McElveen
Jeronia McClish
Janie S. McCullough
Carolyn Maddox McKee
Mary H. McLeod
Ameenah K. McMillan
Barbara McNeal
Lillie Mae Minter
Geneva Moore
Bobbie W. Moorehead
Hattie M. Morris
Shirley Ann Davis Morris

Carol Moseley-Braun
Emily Calloway Mosely
Kathleen Mosley
Kimya Moyo
Melba Mullins
Mary Julia Murray
Mary L. Murray
Dorothy "Ree" DuBose
    Myles
Willena Nanton
Margaret Napier
Esther Napier Alli
Armentha Nesbitt
Jeanne L. Noble
Vera Norman Whisenton
Joan Odom
Margaret Girton O'Neal
Georgia A. Overton
Jacquelyn Heath Parker
Kimberly Dawn Parker
Rosa L. Parks
Hilda R. Pemberton
Mary H. Pershay
Grace Walker Phillips
Alethia B. Porter
Alvin F. Poussaint
Valorie Powell
Harriet Powell
Connie Strachan Questell
Irma Ramsey-Cuellar
Angela E. Randall
Doris J. "Doll" Randall
Rose Elizabeth Sells Rhetta
Barbara Brown Richardson
Mary J. Richardson
LaVerne V. Robinson
Mattilyn Corelia Rochester
Mattilyn Talford Rochester
Ellen Robinson Rolfes
Zandra R. Rucker
Dawn A. Russell
La Veria Ann Sanders
Enid G. Sargeant
Autrilla Watkins Scott
Rosetta L. Scott
Marci Scott
Cilla Seely
Doris Seely
Julie Seely
Melanie Rhodes Shelwood
Dorothy Shepard
Rachel Adjoa Siriboe
Odessa L. Skeene
Barbara J. Skinner
Brenda A. B. Smith
Nellie J. Smith
Rosita Soler
Joyce D. Sowells
Marie H. Stellos

Dorothy L. Stevenson
Waverly Stewart
Steven Stewart
Daria L. Dillard Stone
Lucy Cooper Summers
Rose Marie Dickens
    Swanson
Claudette Francois Sweet
Niara Sudarkasa
Ellen Szunyogh
Susan L. Taylor
Bennie Mae Thomas
Betty Thomas
Lucile Thomas
Lettie Ann Thompson
Maezell Thurman
Christine Toney
Theresa Trainer
Gloria Tribble
Jovis Tuggle
Janet T. Turner
Barbara VanBlake
Thelma Vernelle Upperman
Margie Wade
Pam Waldrop
Frances L. Walker
Leonidis H. Walker
Jeni Wallace
Jessie Davis Walls
Jeannine Ward
Maxine Waters
Rolonda Watts
Carolyn L. Weaver
Princess Weaver
Eva Webster
Shirley J. Wells
Elizabeth P. West
Vera Norman Whisenton
Barbara L. White
Marilyn E. White
Nola Lancaster Whiteman
Lois Whiteside
Ora Lee Wilbarger
Vivian Wiley
Adeline M. Williams
Bobbie J. Oliver Williams
Minerva Williams
Novell Williams
Johnnie Mae Wilson
Nancy Wilson
Letitia "Tish" Winfield
Oris Winslow-Dukes
Renetta T. Womack-Howard
Betty Woodson
Jeanne D. Woodson
Esther Wynn
Margaret Yarbrough
Carol Yates-Bennett

INDEX

CELEBRATING OUR MOTHERS' KITCHENS

National Council of Negro Women, Inc.
c/o Wimmer Cookbook Distribution
4210 B. F. Goodrich Blvd.
Memphis, TN 38118

Please send ___ copies of *Celebrating Our Mothers' Kitchens*

@ $15.95 each _____

Tennessee residents add sales tax @ $1.32 each _____

Postage and handling @ $3.00 each _____

TOTAL _____

Charge to Visa ( ) or MasterCard ( ) # _____

Exp. Date _____

Signature _____

Name _____

Address _____

City _____ State _____ Zip _____

Make checks payable to **Wimmer Cookbook Distribution**
OR CALL: 1(800) 727-1034 OR FAX: (901) 795-9806

- -

CELEBRATING OUR MOTHERS' KITCHENS

National Council of Negro Women, Inc.
c/o Wimmer Cookbook Distribution
4210 B. F. Goodrich Blvd.
Memphis, TN 38118

Please send ___ copies of *Celebrating Our Mothers' Kitchens*

@ $15.95 each _____

Tennessee residents add sales tax @ $1.32 each _____

Postage and handling @ $3.00 each _____

TOTAL _____

Charge to Visa ( ) or MasterCard ( ) # _____

Exp. Date _____

Signature _____

Name _____

Address _____

City _____ State _____ Zip _____

Make checks payable to **Wimmer Cookbook Distribution**
OR CALL: 1(800) 727-1034 OR FAX: (901) 795-9806